Read It Right and
Remember What You Read

ABOUT THE AUTHOR

Samuel Smith received the degrees of A.M. and Ph.D. from New York University. He has held positions as research assistant for the New York State Board of Regents' Inquiry into the Character and Cost of Public Education; supervisor and director of research for government programs of adult education; research director and co-author of the National Achievement Tests; and editor of the Dryden Press Handbooks of Physics, Psychology, Educational Psychology, and Sociology. He was formerly head of the Editorial Department of Barnes & Noble, Inc.

Dr. Smith is co-author of *Supervision in the Elementary School* and *Education and Society,* a contributor to *Principles of Sociology* and *Educational Psychology* in Barnes & Noble's College Outline Series, and co-author of *Best Methods of Study,* also in the College Outline Series.

EVERYDAY HANDBOOKS

Read It Right and Remember What You Read

Samuel Smith

BARNES & NOBLE, INC. NEW YORK

Publishers · Booksellers · Since 1873

Distributed

In Canada
   by McGraw-Hill Company of Canada Ltd.,
   Toronto

In Australia and New Zealand
   by Hicks, Smith & Sons Pty. Ltd.,
   Sydney and Wellington

In the United Kingdom, Europe,
and South Africa
   by Chapman & Hall Ltd., London

Printed in the United States of America

Dedicated to

students, teachers, booksellers, and librarians, whose integrity, competent hands, and discerning minds are preserving the values and reshaping the destiny of modern society

Preface

The purpose of this book is to assist adult readers to become expert readers of newspapers, documents, and books of every description, including poetry, plays, essays, and fiction. Numerous practical suggestions are presented relating to the main aspects of reading: how to test one's speed and comprehension; how to remember what has been read; how to analyze and deal with propaganda and obtain accurate information; how to find and use printed materials most efficiently; how to read contracts and protect one's legal rights; how to read, understand, and enjoy the best works of literature; and how to build a personal home library of worthwhile books, including the classical masterpieces of the past and recent books in literature, philosophy, psychology, religion, science, and the arts. It is my conviction that fair-minded, critical reading is the basis for straight thinking. Furthermore, the quality and extent of critical reading in a community are a sure barometer of its moral and spiritual condition. Critical reading is the pathway to respect for knowledge, for the truth, and for the dignity and worth of the individual.

I am grateful to Miss Frances Caplan, of the Barnes & Noble Editorial Department, for helpful emendations; to the Honorable Harold Roegner, for reviewing the section on the reading of contracts; and especially to Mrs. Peggy Fagin, for reading the manuscript and contributing numerous constructive criticisms and suggestions.

CONTENTS

1
How Well Do You Read?

Printed words are only marks on paper until some thoughtful reader gives them meaning. They are nothing but commonly accepted cues to ideas. To communicate in any language, people must agree on the ideas which their words signify. They could define the moon as a wheel of cheese, but they would have to accept the new meaning in order to understand the statement. Moreover, separate words are not the whole story, for the reader must interpret groups of words, such as phrases and clauses. He must examine word relationships so that the entire word pattern conveys the logical and precise message intended by the writer. This task of interpretation requires skills which can be developed only through years of listening, speaking, writing, and reading. Even a lifetime of reading in a single field, such as literature, will not insure perfection. For example, after three and a half centuries of study, scholars are still trying to find out exactly what Shakespeare meant by many passages in his masterpieces. His work remains a potent influence on our language and ways of thinking, but drastic changes in human experience have dulled or distorted the sharp edges of his felicitous "husbandry."

The efficient reader concentrates on the ideas which he himself must *read into* the words. He recognizes and assigns customary meanings to familiar words in a sentence, and he interprets the words as logically connected groups expressing ideas. He does not stop to explore the implications of every word, but he is alert to the organization of the words and notices how they function as subjects, predicates, objects, prepositions, and conjunctions. He cannot expect merely to look at words and absorb their meanings without thinking; instead he must react sensitively to the words and sentences, since what he gets *out* of them will depend upon the intelligent thought he invests *in* them. He can feel relaxed, enjoying every sentence without tension, yet he must think straight and concentrate on meanings. Clear thinking will reward him with full understanding and appreciation of the writer's message.

On the other hand, superficiality—the quick-and-easy attitude—is a great handicap. For this reason the problem of reading improvement is a moral one; efficient reading requires self-direction, self-discipline, a positive, receptive attitude toward the feelings and ideas of other people. Excessive speed and careless thinking go together. Both must be avoided.

Reading efficiency depends primarily upon the number of ideas per minute that are clearly understood by the reader; or more precisely, it depends upon speed and comprehension.

SPEED

It has become the custom in our society to hurry recklessly from one task to another, often creating new problems instead of really solving the old ones. Without stopping to think, to evaluate our activities, we waste our most precious possession—the time of our lives—on trivia. Less speed and more straight thinking would go far to prevent or remedy many of the world's ills.

Excessive speed in reading, as in driving a car or in performing any other everyday activity, is likely to bring regrettable consequences. Too many of us try to accomplish too much too quickly. In literature and the arts, genuine understanding, enjoyment, and appreciation take time. The reckless driver wrecks his car to save a few worthless seconds. Just as foolish is the man who marches through an art gallery in half an hour, boasting that he has seen scores of paintings any one of which requires careful scrutiny for genuine *seeing*. We need only look about us to witness the consequences of thought-less haste which produce nothing but confusion and tur-moil in our private lives and public business.

What is excessive reading speed? What is the most reasonable and effective rate? Is it 400 or 1,000 or 3,000 words per minute? Whenever the reader fails to under-stand clearly what the writer has written reading speed is excessive. A rate too fast for one may be slow for other readers better prepared to comprehend the material. Consider, for example, the following sentence:

> *Everything which exists, exists either in itself*
> *or in something else.*

The words in this sentence can be read in less than three seconds, yet the sentence is difficult to understand and involves so many implications for the average reader that he could usefully devote an hour of serious thinking to it. The quotation is from *The Ethics* of Spinoza. All the words on any page of that volume could be read in one minute, but for most readers (who are not philoso-phers) that would be the most inefficient way to read the book. With material requiring close attention, a rate of 300 words per minute might be very fast, even for sentences consisting of short, simple words. Surely it is better to lose a few moments by reading (and thinking) carefully than it is to rush through the page with only a vague or imperfect understanding of the writer's message.

If you usually read a newspaper at the rate of 300 or more words per minute, without hurrying, and if you also understand clearly what you are reading, you need not worry about your reading speed. It will be satisfac-tory for most purposes. To test yourself, count 300 words in any newspaper column and time your reading. If you finish in less than one minute, your rate is acceptable. But if you require much more time, perhaps 80 seconds or more, to read the material with full understanding, it is possible that some bad habits are slowing you down. Among the most common of these are lip movements, finger pointing, head turning, regressive movements, and word-by-word reading.

Lip Movements. Moving the lips (or subvocalization) is a frequent cause of slow reading. If you consider the differences between oral and silent reading, the significance of this bad habit will become clear. First, since the eyes move faster than the lips, silent reading can be accomplished much faster than oral reading. Pronouncing one or several words as you read will waste time and reduce your rate. Second, subvocalization interrupts your eye movements and thus compels you to read almost as slowly as in oral reading. Lip movements distract your attention from the onward sweep of the eyes and make it difficult for you to grasp the meaning of each sentence as a whole. If you keep your lips still and closed, giving all your attention to one complete group of words, you will be able to go on promptly to the next group, then to the next, and so on. Third, because lip movements force you to emphasize individual words within a sentence, you may not see immediately the connections between one complete sentence and all the other sentences in a paragraph. Finally, since lip movements tend to scatter your attention among the separate words, you may have to reread more often in order to understand each phrase and paragraph as a whole.

Occasional use of lip movements does not, however, require drastic corrective measures. On the contrary, if used sparingly, subvocalization may help you appreciate fully the writer's emphasis and true meaning. Better still is oral reading. Steady, uninterrupted silent reading at a fixed rate can become monotonous, tiresome, and inefficient. At such times, a change to oral reading can be particularly effective. The relative slowness of oral reading gives you time to think carefully while reading aloud and to derive the precise meaning intended by the writer.

Robert Frost, one of America's most gifted poets and minds of the past, wisely advised readers to listen to sentence sounds, the imagined sounds of the words they are silently reading:

> I have known people who could read without hearing the sentence sounds and they are the fastest readers. Eye readers we call them. They can get the meaning by glances. But they are bad readers because they miss the best part of what a good writer puts into his words. You listen for the sentence sounds. If you find some of those not bookish caught fresh from the mouths of people, some of them striking, all of them definite and recognizable, so recognizable that with a little trouble you can place them and even name them, you know you have found a writer. (From Margaret Bartlett Anderson, *Robert Frost and John Bartlett*, published by Holt, Rinehart and Winston.)

However, if lip movements in silent reading are excessive, the real cause may be lack of concentration. If you concentrate on the idea behind a group of words, you will be less apt to stop at every word. Feel free to try oral reading or a minimum of deliberate lip movements to counteract boredom or fatigue—to break the monotony and give yourself a fresh start—but go back to faster silent reading as soon as possible.

Finger Pointing. Do you point a finger at the words you are reading? If so, you are probably reducing your rate and impeding your comprehension. This habit may indicate a failure to concentrate on the material or lack of interest in it; the reader points at the words as if to force himself onward. The remedy is to keep the fingers busy holding the edges of the page and turning the pages. As you read, move your eyes steadily from one group of words to the next. Finger pointing has the same bad effects as excessive lip movements, and the two habits frequently go together. Eliminate them in most of your reading by giving all your attention to eye movements and to the ideas being expressed in each sentence.

Head Turning. Perhaps you have observed someone who as he reads turns his head from side to side, using his head as a pointer to keep track of the words. This is another bad habit easily corrected. Eye movements are faster than head movements, as a rule. Therefore, head turnings can slow a reader down and distract his attention from ideas in the material. If you make these head movements, stop at once and reread the same material, but this time keep your head rigid as your eyes move along the lines and concentrate on the meaning behind each group of words.

Regressive Movements. Another difficulty arises when a reader, usually one who is in too much of a hurry, misses a point which is necessary for correct understanding of the thought in a sentence. He must then go back to reread the entire sentence. Not only does this waste time but, since the eyes traverse the same ground twice, it often interrupts his effort to follow the trend of ideas. The reader has to reject a partial or incorrect meaning and then grasp the corrected meaning. All of this interrupts the flow of his reading and distracts his attention from the writer's message.

Regressive movements tend to increase if the reading material is unfamiliar or poorly organized, or if the reader loses interest in it. The more he has to go back over what he has missed, the more impatient and bored he becomes, thus increasing further the number of regressive movements. Often it is best at this stage to abandon the attempt to read for a brief interval or to try oral reading. If you decide later that the writer's ideas are worth your time, you can resume silent reading and concentrate on his ideas again. Consider, however, whether some of the difficulty might not be of your own making. Perhaps you need to prepare yourself by obtaining a better background of information before reading the material. You may have read too slowly, owing perhaps to excessive worry about possibly missing a minor point here and there, or maybe you have hurried through the important material and thus missed essential points which would cast a different light on the entire work.[1] If you discipline yourself to read carefully but steadily forward and to think about the writer's ideas, you may develop enthusiastic interest. React to what you read, even if only to discuss it with a friend. What we get out of reading depends on what we put into it; needed are serious attention, a sympathetic, receptive attitude, a willingness to think and feel deeply, with liberal use of the imagination. All these things help to increase enthusiasm for reading, and enthusiastic interest impels the reader to progress from one idea to the next without excessive, boring repetition.

Word-by-Word Reading. The reader's eyes should take in a meaningful group of words at a glance, not stopping at each word. Some readers habitually read one word at a time as if they hoped to build up the writer's idea by adding one word to the next. That is a tiresome, inefficient method of reading. The obvious remedy is to look at a group of words at each glance so that the emphasis will be placed on their meaning as an organized set or unit. Readers vary as to their grouping of words within a sentence, but such variations do not matter. Most important is the need for some logical grouping which will bring out the connections among words and make the intended ideas clear.

Variable Speed. In writing music the composer usually includes directions to musicians: for example, *ritardando* is a direction to play more slowly, and *presto* to play rapidly. Since reading materials do not contain such instructions, the reader must adjust his rate of reading to the type of material and to his purpose in reading. He has to bear in mind the degree of understanding he wishes

---

[1] If you are reading a legal contract, an insurance policy, or a similar vital document, be sure to read it as often as necessary before accepting it, because misunderstanding some of the shortest words or missing them could have disastrous consequences. Take plenty of time, ask questions, supplement silent reading with slow oral reading, and get expert advice on any vague or dubious clauses.

to achieve. If he desires only a quick, general idea of what the material is about, he can hurry his reading until he finds out. But if he wants a full understanding, he will devote enough time for careful, thorough reading and thinking. The claim that fast readers also comprehend best what they read may be true, but the reason is their efficient reading habits, not their speed.[2] A slow reader who attempts to increase his rate by hurrying may discover that he has become less efficient, and his comprehension may suffer unless he concentrates on understanding clearly what he reads, regardless of his rate. Comprehension must therefore be the basic consideration for all readers.

COMPREHENSION

In recent decades it has become the fashion to analyze reading comprehension as consisting of four elements: word meaning, sentence meaning, details, and paragraph meaning. This kind of analysis has been widely used by psychologists to measure reading efficiency. Another type of analysis is based on the actual experience of the reader as he reacts to printed material. Such an analysis emphasizes the following elements: preparation for reading; the structure of the reading material; relative difficulty of the material; reactions of the reader to the material. The following discussions will clarify the factors affecting comprehension and help you to evaluate your own efficiency.

Speed and Comprehension. First, however, let us repeat the point that thinking—ideas—should be made the central focus in reading. Reading advisers claim that they can help anyone double his reading rate and at the same time improve his comprehension. They then may attempt to train the reader to move his eyes faster or to hurry through page after page of material. But we should note

---

[2] To measure your normal rate of book reading, take the speed test on page 212.

the practical significance of the first sentence in this chapter: Printed words are only marks on paper until some thoughtful reader gives them meaning. The reader recognizes a group of words as a unit only because he has seen the same symbols repeatedly; as he reads he deliberately concentrates on interpreting them. In other words, seeing is a form of thinking. The entire emphasis must therefore be placed on the idea, the meaning, inherent (or customarily assumed to be inherent) in each group of words. The reader may choose to interpret at a glance a smaller or a larger group of words, but his choice should always be based upon the thoughts (concepts) he forms as he responds to the material. Of course, his thinking and imagination cannot run wild—he cannot really remake the moon into cheese or discover meaningful words in nonsense syllables. Yet the actual limitations on his thinking are self-imposed—the result of repeated experience with the meanings of words during a lifetime of learning. A single letter or word may be significant, although most often it must be seen as joined with other letters and words for efficient interpretation. These relationships take time to be noted and appreciated. The rate of reading should never be so high as to interfere with the degree of understanding desired by the reader.

If fast readers comprehend what they read better than slow readers, should slow readers try to speed up in order to improve their comprehension? Not at all, because the more probable result would be that the slow readers would become more careless if they tried to rush through their reading materials. But if slowness is due to certain bad habits, slow readers can benefit permanently from attempts to achieve a faster rate by eliminating the bad habits. The same good habits which insure acceptable reading speed can also help the reader to achieve better understanding. Thus, if the reader forms the habit of looking for the most significant words in a sentence and grouping them with subordinate words in a meaningful whole, he will quickly grasp the correct ideas and promptly move ahead to the next sentence. Obviously, if he understands the meaning of a clause at once, he can proceed without a stop to the next clause and increase his speed. The development of good reading habits of this kind (in contrast to the bad habits developed by poor readers) explains why many rapid readers are superior to slow readers in comprehension. In any case, understanding, not speed, should be the primary aim.

Second, therefore, let us review briefly the main elements to be considered in achieving adequate comprehension at a reasonable speed.

Word Meaning. How well you read depends in part upon your vocabulary, your storehouse of word meanings. Developing a rich vocabulary can be complicated because many English words have a variety of meanings, depending on their context. The word *get*, for example, has scores of meanings, some of them readily seen in the following sentences:

> Get well. Get me some food. Get along with him. Do you get the idea? Get started. Get her out of trouble. Get over your illness. Get in the house. Get to him by telephone. Get ahead of him. Get down. Get loose. Get together.

Since the meaning of a word is often changed through its relationship to nearby words, the reader must choose the best meaning in each case; and he may misinterpret the sentence if he makes an incorrect choice. Rarely is it sufficient to know only one or two meanings of a word. Instead, the reader should gain real mastery of all the important meanings. An excellent way to do this is to read a variety of books written by competent authors, past and present. Reading the same words in numerous writings will acquaint the reader with their different meanings or shades of meaning.

The greatest difficulty in understanding words comes from excessive speed. If you read too fast, you are likely to interpret some words incorrectly or not quite so clearly as you should. Thus the entire material may seem to you to imply a meaning not intended by the author. To think carefully about the different possible meanings of a word requires time, and this requirement makes excessive speed unwise. Take plenty of time to think of the most likely meanings of a word whenever you have any doubt as to its meaning in a particular sentence. (The test of word discrimination on page 215 will help you to evaluate this phase of your vocabulary. Other phases are discussed in the next chapter.) If you have an extensive vocabulary and read attentively, you will not have to stop too often or reread too many words and sentences.

Sentence Meaning. A single word may be an entire sentence: *Assuredly. Certainly.* Or a sentence may consist of many words organized into logical groups such as phrases and clauses.

> Are you going so early in the morning?
> When I asked what is matter, he replied, "Never mind," but when I asked what is mind, he replied, "No matter."

It is difficult to decide upon the main ideas in these sentences, because the reader has to consider a number of possible ideas and compare one with the others. These ideas depend largely upon key words in each sentence. If, therefore, you notice the meanings of the key words—those which contribute most to a main idea—you will more readily understand the sentence as a whole. Further, most sentences follow or precede others. If you take care to make the connections linking these sentences, you will more easily interpret each of them correctly. Obviously, if you make a mistake in reading a sentence, but remember that the resulting idea would contradict what you have already read in a preceding sentence, you will reread both sentences carefully to solve the discrepancy. In this way, you use each newly read sentence as a check, a bit of evidence, concerning the probable meanings of the other sentences. Finally, since most of the longer sentences you read will contain one main idea with minor ideas grouped around it, you should note this organization within a sentence and make certain that it is logical.

Details. During their experimental work and testing in the past fifty years, researchers have discovered that readers might grasp the main idea of a sentence or a paragraph, yet might miss or misunderstand minor points of information. Just as there is a tendency for certain slow readers to encounter difficulty with the major ideas and the logical connections among groups of words, so there is a temptation for some faster readers to overlook details. This relationship between main ideas and subordinate information in reading material is, however, still largely unexplored. In some material the details are closely related to the principal idea and may, in fact, lead up to it or clarify its meaning. As a practical matter, the reader should ask himself what he wishes to gain from his reading of the material and should adjust his rate and attention accordingly. If, for example, he wishes to make sure he knows every step in the writer's exposition, he will have to read slowly enough for this purpose, but if he is willing to overlook some minor points on the assumption that omitting them will not affect his interpretation of the main thesis, he can skim them rapidly and go on to the next major idea.

Paragraph Meaning. Most reading materials are organized into paragraphs. Students are told that a typical paragraph contains a single topic discussed in a group of sentences. Writers who are proficient usually organize their works in accordance with this pattern. Nevertheless, readers sometimes have difficulty deciding whether a given paragraph deals with one central idea or with two or more ideas, each of equal or nearly equal significance. The expert grammarian may insist that equivalent ideas should be discussed in separate paragraphs, but the writer may wish to treat them together as a unit in a logically knit group of sentences. Moreover, too many writers display unawareness of grammatical principles in their work. Consequently, the reader must be careful to notice all the main ideas in each paragraph and judge for himself their relationship to sentences within the paragraph and to adjacent paragraphs.

Successive paragraphs, of course, comprise the bulk of reading materials. The skilled reader notes the large topic covered by all these paragraphs in a chapter or section. He looks for a logical or chronological organization as he reads. Bearing in mind what has gone before, he tackles each paragraph while anticipating what he may discover next, and he constantly derives satisfactions either when his expectations are verified by the material or when he is pleasantly surprised by the writer's variations, digressions, and new ideas.[3]

Preparation for Reading. If you were asked to read a novel in a language entirely unfamiliar to you, even the first word would probably mystify you. In all reading, you must have had some experience with both the language and the subject. Yet many readers assume that they can read any material without preparation; for this reason they often form an inaccurate or imperfect impression of the material. As you begin to read, surely you can at least think back to your reading experiences of the past, review information or reawaken memories, and thus enrich or improve your understanding of the new material.

There are two special ways in which the reader's previous reading and experience can help his immediate reading: comparison to note similarities; and contrast to note differences. The reader asks himself, Does what I am reading agree with the things I have read about the same subject? Is the main idea logical and true if judged on the basis of my life experience? What are the strong and the weak points in the material? If the reader has prepared himself well by means of extensive varied reading on the subject and asks these questions as he reads, he will reach a high level of reading efficiency.

The old saying "he who has, gets more" holds good for reading. The person who has read more widely and effi-

---

[3] As we shall see, skill in reading successive paragraphs can be developed. Meanwhile, note that on page 220 there is a test on paragraph meaning which will help you to evaluate your own skill in this central aspect of reading.

ciently and who has enjoyed a rich life experience gets more out of each new reading activity. But it is never too late to make up for neglect of reading, and anyone can easily set aside time, no matter how busy he is, for a regular program of daily reading. The more one reads, the better he is prepared for further reading.

Structure of the Reading Material. Although reading materials are usually organized well enough to give the reader a number of clues or directions to guide his thinking and feeling, they also leave ample scope for use of his imagination and powers of interpretation. Two readers may interpret the same paragraphs quite differently. The meaning of a single sentence or, for that matter, the main point of an entire book may vary widely with different readers. Even expert critics may arrive at opposite conclusions about the writer's purpose and accomplishment. Furthermore, on some important points a few of the foremost authorities may agree with the novice attempting literary criticism. Works of great writers, such as Shakespeare, have been misinterpreted as much by scholars as by unschooled tyros.

Nevertheless, the writer generally organizes his sentences, paragraphs, and chapters sufficiently to provide the reader with considerable guidance in comprehension. There may be a logical or chronological sequence of ideas, or some other systematic arrangement, such as comparison and contrast, development from simple to complex propositions, and organized patterns of introductory, main, subordinate, and concluding sections. With fiction, the reader may note special narrative techniques such as flashbacks, which may require patience and discrimination on his part if he wishes to gain full appreciation of the material.

Difficulty of the Reading Material. It is possible to construct a check list of the things which make reading materials difficult and to rate the materials on a scale of relative difficulty. But what is almost unintelligible to most people might be perfectly simple to readers expert in a special field, such as mathematics or science, music or philosophy, medicine or other professions. The meaning of what is being read today depends upon what has been read, thought, and lived before today. In estimating the difficulty of reading material, one must consider not only the average number of words in sentences, the lengths of the words and sentences, and the complexity of structure, but especially the extent to which the ideas being presented involve or hinge upon the reader's previous reading and experience.

Reactions of the Reader. The best test of understanding is the reaction of the reader to the reading material—what he thinks and does in response to his interpretation. Thus, if he is reading directions, his understanding will be reflected in the way he follows them. If he is reading abstract ideas, his comprehension will be indicated by what he says, thinks, or writes about the ideas. Even when you arrive at incorrect conclusions about what you read, your discussion of the topic will reflect the extent of your understanding; that is, your conclusions will at least be based, rightly or wrongly, on an intelligent grasp of some of the ideas you have read.

2
How To Improve
Your Reading

There is so much to read—books, letters, documents, newspapers, and magazines—that in the limited time available to them many people would like to increase their reading rate in order to absorb more information and ideas. Even the best reader may at times wish to cover more ground if he can do so without misunderstanding what he is reading. Fortunately, psychologists investigating methods of reading which combine high speed and full comprehension have contributed suggestions for reading improvement, some of them temporarily effective, others more lasting and satisfactory. An average reader, so they claim, could double or even triple his reading rate by means of special training and new techniques.

Recently machines have been invented which keep track of the reader's eye movements and help him to eliminate wasteful or careless ways of scanning printed words. Some experts have recommended devices which impel the reader to move his eyes quickly in the proper direction across the page as well as backward and downward from one line to the next. Thus by looking only at the middle part of a group of words, the reader automatically sees the other words, too, and is able to read much more at a glance instead of looking at words in sequence. When psychologists administer tests to readers who have practiced methods such as these, the results often appear to be gratifying. Of course, some readers score high on the tests because they have become adept at taking tests, not necessarily because they have improved their natural reading habits, and in many instances the apparent progress gained through special training disappears when the reader goes back to his old habits or stops trying to read as fast as possible. In fact, concentrating on speed and using devices to increase reading rate may eventually interfere with reading efficiency, which depends upon close attention to the reading material itself.

There are, however, certain effective ways to improve one's natural reading rate and comprehension. Previewing is one of them.

PREVIEWING

It is easy to form the habit of previewing what you intend to read. Previewing is like studying a map before starting on a journey. The map discloses how far you will probably have to travel, where you may stop to rest or to reconsider your route and schedule, where you will have to choose among alternative routes, and speed limits and other conditions of the journey.

Previews of reading material vary in scope from a quick glance at headings and selected sentences to a rather detailed yet rapid skimming of selected parts of the material. You can make good use of previews as preparation for more careful reading of any kind of written or printed text—correspondence, news, feature articles, and fiction or non-fiction books. Previews will help you to adjust your reading speed to the difficulty of the material. On the basis of an adequate preview, you may decide to skip some portions and to concentrate on others, or you may prefer to study every paragraph carefully.

The following group of five sentences illustrates one advantage of previewing.

1. The efficient reader must be logical.
2. The efficient reader must be logical, alert, and attentive.

3. The efficient reader must be logical, alert, and attentive to ideas.

4. The efficient reader must be logical, alert, and attentive to ideas which the writer intended to communicate.

5. The efficient reader must be logical, alert, and attentive to ideas which the writer intended to communicate and must devote adequate time to insure clear understanding.

Notice that each new sentence was made longer through the addition of a few words. If you read the five sentences separately without becoming aware of the pattern, you probably had to read slowly and stop to think about the ideas in each sentence. But if you quickly examined all the sentences and noticed the pattern, you could merely glance at the first part of each sentence and concentrate on reading the added words. In this way a preview of reading material reveals the pattern, the route to be taken on your reading journey. It provides you with a mental map of what lies ahead so that you can adjust your speed of reading to the material and devote your efforts particularly to the most significant passages.

In the sentences listed above, the pattern is one of similarities and differences. There are numerous other patterns to be found in reading materials: for example, some patterns are based on the structure and form of sentences and paragraphs (as in the use of very brief phrases to separate them); others depend upon the author's use of questions, method of alternating short and long clauses or sentences, interpolation of dialogue, logical development of a main thesis, or unexpected changes in point of view. Even an awareness of undesirable patterns, such as monotonous repetition of arguments or adherence to a cut-and-dried, dull organization of data, may help the alert reader to evaluate, comprehend, and recall the reading material.

As a special advantage, previewing provides the reader with an opportunity to estimate what he can get out of the material before devoting a great deal of time to it. When you preview a few pages, ask yourself what information, pleasure, or other benefit you expect to derive from the text. This question will direct your attention to those parts of the material which will contribute most to the results you desire, such as answers to specific questions, explanations of principles, or ideas which should stimulate your thinking, understanding, and appreciation. A preview of anything from a single page to a whole volume, if followed by careful study, can help you to achieve definite goals in reading.

If you are reading an educational book or textbook, preview the structure of each chapter before beginning a detailed study. Note the chapter title, the main and subordinate headings, the amount of space allotted to various topics, the sequence of topics, the questions, references, and citations, and the charts, diagrams, or other illustrations. Then recall what you already know about the topics of the chapter and formulate questions for which you hope to find the answers in the text.

After you have read one section of a book, preview the next section and ask yourself in what ways the two sections are related to each other. Does the new section supplement, reinforce, or counterbalance the old? Does it introduce a new phase or element of the subject? Noting the connections between ideas already read and new passages to come may increase both speed and comprehension. The old material becomes clearer and more meaningful if it is seen to be related to the new. With short stories and novels, try previewing the plot in your own mind—guessing in advance what events are about to be described. As you continue with more careful reading, you will see how the author either met your expectations or shaped his plot quite differently. You may also recapitulate the main events which have already occurred in the story, decide upon several possible outcomes, and later note which ones the author adopted as well as the probable reasons for his choices. A quick preview of the actual plot, followed by detailed reading, will disclose the pattern of the story as a whole and help you to remember essential parts.

If you are reading a short story or suspense novel for enjoyment, you may prefer to read without previewing, because enjoyment of the plot may depend in part upon a surprise element which previewing could spoil. The reader who looks ahead and discovers how the plot is going to end may find the story less interesting or less challenging when he begins to read it more carefully. On the other hand, if the plot is too complicated, previewing will help to make it more intelligible.

Previewing of newspapers and journals can be useful but entails considerable risk of obtaining only a superficial or inaccurate view of the facts. News and feature articles should not be swallowed but digested. Previewing headlines on various pages, or even rapidly skimming a summary of events, should be nothing more than a preliminary step. To understand a news story or a feature article correctly, to avoid error or distortion, preview to select what you want to read and then read the entire story or article. Read every word of it.

Newspaper makeup follows a traditional pattern which helps the reader to select what he is interested in reading. The editor places the most significant news in the extreme right-hand column of the front page, sometimes with related material in adjacent columns. News which is of secondary importance is located in the column at the extreme left of the front page. Some front-page topics may be continued in the inside pages, in which case it is a mistake to read only the part on the front page; you should read the whole story before turning back to the first page for another selection. Often the continuation on the inside pages will change your idea about a topic.

A newspaper story begins with the most significant event and then explains details which preceded the event. It differs therefore from most other types of reading material, which begin with introductory or descriptive information and gradually lead up to the important event or climax. The headlines and lead sentences in a newspaper story are cues designed to attract the attention of readers who may be in a hurry to get the main facts before deciding whether or not to read further. You can use headlines and lead sentences to decide what to read in greater detail, but be sure to read the entire story to determine the facts.

SKIMMING

Skimming is a special form of previewing—a method of exploring reading materials rapidly without stopping to interpret each clause or sentence but with enough attention to obtain a general view of the theme and its development. Skimming can also locate answers to specific questions, points of information, and ideas which interest the reader. Thus, if you wish to ascertain only one or two facts, you do not have to read large portions of a text or reference work. Look up the relevant topic in the index and skim the pages until you come to the data you need. Then read these selected passages carefully.

Do not be misled by the notion that skimming requires only a glance at a few headings or paragraphs now and then without attention to ideas. On the contrary, skimming requires particular alertness to the material being read to avoid the possibility of missing or misinterpreting the writer's message. You must immediately notice any headings and all key statements in complicated passages, quickly grasping what the headings and statements mean, and you must do this without stopping, while continuing to sweep your eyes across and down the page to additional headings and key statements.

Attentive skimming can show you how different parts of reading material fit together to form a logical structure. You can observe relationships among the principal ideas being presented, how one idea or part leads into the next, and which parts will require the most time and effort. By skimming several parts before reading each you can often discover the plan of a book and in this way avoid a common pitfall of the unskilled reader, that of interpreting passages in the wrong sense, only to find, later on, that his views are inconsistent with another portion of the text. Skimming before careful reading will increase your self-confidence, because as you read the author's first ideas you will remember what is coming next and how these ideas are connected with ideas in other sections of the text.

In skimming you must ascertain which sentences on a page contain the main ideas or the important conclusions. These key sentences may be buried within paragraphs or they may be brief statements separating paragraphs. They may be topic sentences, the ones which state the main ideas (or pinpoint the topics) of the paragraphs. A topic sentence is often placed at or near the beginning of a paragraph but sometimes at the end. It may even be in the form of a question which the paragraph answers in considerable detail. The topic sentence summarizes the main point of the paragraph. An experienced skimmer can skim page after page, locating topic sentences from which he obtains the most significant ideas of the book. With continued practice you will develop skill in finding the topic sentences and other key sentences. Bear in mind, however, that you can seldom expect to get enough information from skimming and will usually find it necessary to reread the material carefully from beginning to end. This will be especially beneficial because by repeating the main ideas (noted while skimming), you will be helped in remembering them. Further, you will be reading them in two different arrangements—first, as separate important points, or highlights, of information and, second, as central ideas around which all the other sentences in each paragraph cluster in such a way as to clarify, reinforce, or supplement those ideas.

Occasionally you may be in a hurry to locate and read information, knowing that you will have only a few moments for this purpose instead of an hour or more required for careful reading. At such times, you may use a technique which, at the risk of some inaccuracy, will facilitate high-speed skimming. Close one eye and as you quickly move the other eye down the page, move the index finger of your right hand steadily downward at the right of the printed lines. Your eye movements will become more rapid as you try to make them keep pace with your moving finger in the margin. As you glance at the sentences, look for key words relating to the information you want. By practicing this technique you can greatly increase your reading rate and skim page after page in a fraction of the normal time. However, owing to the danger of superficial or imperfect comprehension of the reading material, this method should be used only in emergency situations. Never mistake skimming for thorough reading of a book; partial information is no substitute for comprehensive knowledge.

READING FOR IDEAS

Although every word in a sentence represents some kind of idea, a great many ideas depend upon groups of logically connected words each of which contributes something to the total message. We communicate our thoughts to other people, not by separating one word from the next, but rather by combining words into phrases, clauses, sentences, and paragraphs, all of which function as cues to the reader, who must then interpret their author's meanings. The meaning of a single word in a group usually varies with its relationship to its neighbors. Thus the word "fall" in "the fall of Rome" means something quite different from the same word in "the fall is a season of the year."

Seeing things in sets, groups, or clusters, not as independent symbols or units, is a universal experience. We see everything around us as groups of things arranged in some sequence or order. Our eyes are lenses in motion through which we examine the shape of the world, and as our eyes move, we see new groups of things which interest us and have meaning for us. When we recognize a friend, we do not look first at his left eye, then at his right eye, nose, mouth, and head. We see him as a composite the parts of which supplement each other and form a pattern or, as some psychologists call it, a gestalt. The same process occurs in reading. We recognize a word as an ordered arrangement of familiar letters. We then recognize several words as an orderly group, interpret its customary meaning, and move on to examine the next group of words. But our eyes stop for an instant just before we move them forward, and it is during this brief pause that we think about the meaning of the group of words we have just read.

The inefficient reader makes too many stops, and each of his pauses is too long. He often reads only one word at a time. The efficient reader, on the contrary, instead of stopping to think about one word, then the next, and so on, sees at once that some words in a sentence belong together, that they are in a definite sequence and are logically connected to each other.

The inefficient way to read is shown in the following example, in which each slant line indicates a pause:

Our/fathers/brought/forth/a/new/nation.

The sentence above should be read in two word groups, with only one quick stop between them, as follows:

Our fathers brought forth / a new nation.

Here we think about two main ideas: the first is suggested to us by four words, the second by three words. This method of reading sets of words, instead of separate words, saves time and makes the meaning of the whole sentence simple and clear.

It may help you to read words in groups if you keep in mind the typical order and organization of words in English sentences. In the sentence above, the words are organized grammatically into the subject (Our fathers), the predicate (brought forth), and the object (a new nation). In a flash you can read the subject and the predicate together (the first four words) and then in another quick glance the object (the last three words), which carries the first idea forward.

The following sentence is more difficult to read:

A square circle must exist, / at least in our minds, / because we can think about it.

A skilled reader will read this sentence quickly, making

only two very brief stops. The two commas help him to see that the sentence consists of three groups of words. A glance at the first group (five words) reveals one main idea; it is a strange idea containing the contradictory notion of a "square circle." The next group (five words) modifies the first meaning by adding another idea (that the thought of a square circle exists). The last group (six words) ends the sentence with an explanation (the reason why), an idea which carries the first two ideas forward and completes the entire proposition. Thus, all three groups of words together form a meaningful sentence which the efficient reader can read and interpret quickly with only two brief pauses.

If you keep looking for meanings as you read, concentrating on the ideas in each sentence, you will soon form the habit of reading for ideas and will seldom, if ever, stop for word-by-word reading.

MAKING SENSE OUT OF WORDS

Some words are so familiar to us that we have no difficulty interpreting their mutual relationships in a sentence, easily noting their correct meanings. But other words seem only vaguely familiar or appear to be altogether unknown. Sometimes, too, we mistake one word for another, perhaps because of similar spelling or appearance. The careful reader must be alert to discriminate among words he is sure about, those he is in doubt about, and those which he is sure he does not know.

There is no such thing as an unimportant word, though some words may be more significant than others in a particular sentence. Consider, for instance, the following two sentences:

Put the money in the desk.
Put the money on the desk.

The tiny words "in" and "on" are extremely important, for they can change the meaning of the whole sentence. How often people sign contracts or other documents without noticing the little words, such as "in," "on," "not," "or," "if," and the like! In most kinds of reading, however, the words you will be especially concerned about are those which seem indefinite or difficult for you to interpret— perhaps because you have not read them often enough to insure thorough understanding of their various meanings.

Many readers have trouble with words which they seldom encounter or use; the less frequently a word is heard, read, or spoken, the more difficult its comprehension is likely to be. Repeated and correct usage of a word in its various meanings will make it so familiar that no longer will you have to stop and think about the best possible meaning when you see it in a sentence; you will know immediately how it fits into and adds to the meaning of the entire sentence. In fact, the best way to enlarge your reading vocabulary is to write down unfamiliar or difficult words when you read them or shortly thereafter and later make use of them when speaking or writing until you feel certain that you will never forget their meanings.

Avoid excessive guessing. Too many readers merely guess at the meaning of a somewhat unfamiliar word instead of consulting a dictionary for several possible meanings from which to select the correct one. Let us suppose you feel uncertain about the meaning of the word *cosmopolite* when you read it in a sentence: "He traveled in many lands, felt at home everywhere, and became a true cosmopolite." We could guess from the context that *cosmopolite* in this sentence refers to a person whose interests and sympathies extend to people far beyond his national attachments. In fact, the dictionary tells us that the word comes from two Greek words: *kosmos*, meaning world, and *politēs*, meaning citizen. The precise meaning is, therefore, "citizen of the world." To remember this meaning of *cosmopolite* permanently, you need only construct many sentences using the word correctly in this sense. For such vocabulary building, you should keep a loose-leaf notebook or an alphabetical card file in which to write all the difficult words you read. You do not always have to interrupt your reading to do this, but try to jot down these words at intervals or during pauses in your reading. Later, preferably once or twice a week, practice using your new words in oral and written sentences. Use each word in several of its principal meanings, not limited to the meaning in the original passage containing it. Consult your dictionary to verify the precise meanings of each new word on your list and, whenever you have time, review some of the old words.

If you notice the origins of a word—its sources as given in the dictionary—you will often be able to apply this information to other words derived wholly or partly from the same origins. Thus, if you look up *cosmopolite* in the dictionary and note the Greek origins (*kosmos* and *politēs*), you will have a pretty good idea of the meanings of such English words as *cosmos, cosmopolitan,* and *cosmopolis,* and you will have a clue to part of the meaning of *cosmology* (from the Greek *kosmos* and *logos,* meaning law) and *cosmography* (from the Greek *kosmos* and *graphein,* meaning to write) when you encounter these words in your reading. There is usually sense in words, including highly technical terms, but often you have to dig in to find the sense. Thus, it may be helpful to notice that *cosmotron* is based on the same Greek word *kosmos* and the suffix *tron* (as in neutron, electron, dynatron, and bevatron); but beware of slight yet significant differences in the origins of similar words—for example, *proton* may seem to resemble *neutron* but is spelled with *ton,* not *tron,* and actually is derived from an altogether different Greek word *prōton,* meaning first, a basic combining form in *protocol, protophloem, protoplasm, prototype,* and *protozylem.*

A linguist can analyze parts of a word and explain what each part contributes to the meaning of the whole word in its setting or context, its function in a sentence. When he looks at the word *unkempt,* for instance, he knows that the prefix *un* means not, that *kempt* comes from the Scottish word for comb, and that therefore *unkempt* must mean "not combed" or disordered, disheveled. You do not have to become a linguist in order to read most kinds of printed matter with satisfactory understanding, but the more you know about some of the common prefixes and suffixes, the easier it will be for you to comprehend unfamiliar words.

Suppose you did not know the meaning of the word *exanimate*. You could probably quickly figure out its meaning in a sentence from the prefix *ex,* which means "out of," and *animate,* which refers to life or a life-giving quality; *exanimate* must therefore mean "out of life" or lifeless. But check your interpretation of such words in a dictionary as soon as convenient, for it is easy to choose the wrong meaning. Thus, *anti* means "against" in *antithesis,* but it means "before" or "bygone" in *antiquarian.*

How does a writer enable the reader to obtain new information from the written material? He does this, first, by selecting words which will be widely accepted as denoting relevant ideas or relationships between ideas; and, next, by arranging these words in the proper order so that the reader's thoughts will begin to flow in the same order. The writer thereby gives the reader a start in the desired direction by means of the arrangement of words which both he and the reader comprehend or agree upon, just as a policeman might use sign language or his index finger to direct a traveler to the right road.

Words change their meanings with the times and with the education and cultural backgrounds of writers and readers. The fine distinctions and implications of a word or even the principal meaning may be so altered that it acquires many meanings instead of one or two. The word *politics* has its origin in the same Greek word *politēs,* which means citizen. Originally it referred only to the art of handling public affairs, but in modern times, including most periods of American history, another meaning has developed—stated in Webster's dictionary as "dishonest management to secure the success of candidates or political parties." Changing conditions change definitions. The word *politics* acquired an evil connotation because political leaders on every level of government too often betrayed their trust for selfish ends. There are, of course, political leaders who possess wisdom and integrity, following the examples of Abraham Lincoln, Theodore Roosevelt, and Woodrow Wilson. Nevertheless, for many people politics has come to mean a dirty game suffused with unprincipled chicanery.

Oddly enough, if you are alert when you read, you can sometimes get much more meaning out of a paragraph than the writer intended to put into it. This is particularly evident when a writer makes a poor choice of words. Have you not received letters from a friend who uses the wrong word to express an idea? You may have said to yourself, "He really meant to write something different," and you will think about a number of ways to improve your friend's writing. In the same way a skilled reader can notice deficiencies in printed matter which stimulate his train of thought, perhaps raising questions which the writer did not even intend to discuss and frequently enriching his understanding of the subject. The printed words are then only the starting point for such a reader's reactions as he embellishes and supplements the writer's work. Sometimes an author may undergo a similar experience when he reads his own work after a lapse of time and thinks differently about what he originally wrote. T. S. Eliot did not like the idea of having one of his works reprinted, because he had changed his mind about many topics and did not wish the public to assume he still held steadfast to his old point of view. The alert reader realizes that there is nothing fixed or unalterable about ideas in print, because ideas, like the words expressing them, inevitably change with changing conditions and audiences. The more you react to your reading material, evaluating, interpreting, protesting, doubting, recasting, approving, the more stimulation and benefit you will derive. You will become a better reader and a more sensitive and cultured person.

REINFORCING YOUR READING

Self-confidence is necessary for efficient reading. The confident reader moves steadily forward from one point to another, avoiding excessive doubts or fears about his progress. Readers who lack confidence keep rereading the same sentences and paragraphs and wondering whether they have misunderstood the author's writing and become confused. Too much self-criticism and rereading can be wasteful and damaging. Nevertheless, even the skilled reader can often benefit by certain techniques for organizing, evaluating, and reinforcing what he has read. The most useful of these techniques are rereading, summarizing, underlining, copying, reviewing, and self-testing.

Rereading. A person without confidence in his reading ability tends to go over every printed line because he thinks he may have missed or misunderstood something important. This assumption is a serious mistake which you should so far as possible avoid. Assume instead that you understood what you have read, go on with your reading, and wait until you finish a passage or section before questioning or testing your comprehension. If you stop to check up after every sentence, fearing that you may have misunderstood it, you will not only waste time but will often fail to grasp clearly enough the main idea of the whole paragraph or discussion. Wait until you finish a passage or two before you consider whether you need to reread the material. If you decide to reread, you can then concentrate on making up for anything you missed by giving it more serious attention. When you reread, note especially the words and ideas which you misinterpreted and compare your second interpretation with the first. This self-evaluation will give you a justifiable feeling of self-confidence, for you will know that you have definitely improved your understanding of the writer's message.

Of course, even the most experienced readers sometimes fall short of perfection—a goal you may not achieve but should always aim at. For that matter, expert writers and publishers also make mistakes. Recently on the front page of a highly respected morning newspaper there were several errors which were annoying and confusing. The word *prospective* had been misused for *perspective*. Another sentence had no predicate whatever and was meaningless. In a third sentence there was an illogical comparison between things which cannot be compared. An efficient reader notices and discounts these errors. He will skip the verb-less sentence without wasting time trying to make sense out of it and may pause a moment to wonder at the careless writing of the third sentence before going on to other passages. Such a reader knows what to do, because he has had rich experience in analyzing words, sentence structure, and the logical organization of complex sentences.

Readers must not expect everything they read to be dedicated to high ideals or to be carefully prepared; they must be ready to deal with imperfect work owing to the haste and lack of pride in performance which have become all too common in our society. Fortunately, there are still some competent authors who observe high standards of creative effort, who make it a habit to write in a clear, candid, interesting style for appreciative readers.

Summarizing. After you have read a few pages in a book or perhaps have finished reading a chapter, you may realize that certain ideas (and related facts) therein vary widely in importance, making it difficult for you to organize and discriminate immediately among them. After all, an author may have toiled earnestly preparing a well organized presentation of a single topic, whereas you depend upon one or two quick readings to gain adequate understanding and appreciation of his work. More often than not, he is an expert on the subject, and you are the learner. Nevertheless, if you get into the habit of summarizing carefully what you read, you can often deepen your insight and sometimes even approximate the author's expertise.

Summarizing reverses the procedure used by many skilled authors. They set down ideas and facts in a well organized outline of the main points and relevant evidence or details, and then they simply elaborate upon the listed statements when they write the full text. The reader, on the contrary, begins with the author's final product. If he reads a section and summarizes it carefully, he should end up with something very much like the author's original plan. His summary will disclose how the various parts were fitted together to provide the central meanings and supporting elements of the discussion.

But summarizing well is no easy task. It requires hard and straight thinking. Whether you summarize mentally, without writing, or take notes in the form of an outline or essay, you must apply yourself with care, patience, logic, and system, and with discrimination and sensitivity to values. First, try to recall all the key ideas in what you have read and consider the order or sequence in which they were presented. Which came at or near the beginning, and how was it introduced? Which came last, and what were the points or concepts leading up to it? Which, if any, important ideas were developed between the first and the last? If you decide to write an outline of the material, set down the main ideas, facts, or principles, leaving space for supporting statements and details.

An acceptable outline of the first part of this chapter is shown in the following example:

Introductory: Caution about Speed and Comprehension

Ways to Improve Reading

    Previewing
      Nature
      Advantages
      Textbooks
      Fiction
      Newspapers and journals
    Skimming
      Nature

Advantages
Techniques
   Key sentences
   Finger movements
Reading for Ideas
   Words and ideas
   Words in a pattern
   Word groups as ideas
Making Sense out of Words
   Relativity of word meanings
   Importance of small words
   Interpretation of word meanings
Reinforcing Your Reading
   Rereading
   Summarizing

Each main topic is followed by two or more subtopics. A subdivided main idea has at least two supporting ideas. For each topic the supporting subtopics are equally indented and have the same grammatical structure. This system makes it easy to see the entire framework of a discussion at a glance.

In writing a summary or an outline, you have to decide how many ideas and details of the original material you should include. Summarizing is not a process of merely restating information; it is a distillation of the original material, a result of careful analysis of its ideas and their interrelationships. Putting in too many minor points is just as bad as omitting important ones. If you write complete statements about the main ideas, instead of making a list of topics, your statements should be clear and brief, and the relationship between each important idea and its subordinate ideas should be evident at once.

After completing your summary, go back to the original material, compare the two, and revise your version wherever necessary to insure a full and logical development of the author's ideas. Doing this will often improve your understanding of his work and stimulate your own thinking, and it will certainly help you to remember what you have read.

Underlining. When should the reader underline and what should he underline? Some people refuse to underline any book, claiming that such marking is disfiguring and interferes with another reader's use of the book. To them books are almost sacred possessions to be preserved, never to be marred, not even for their greater enlightenment—but why are books written if not for the benefit of their readers? Others believe that underlining or making notations will increase the value of the book when they first read it and later when they wish to refer to important parts. Most readers find underlining helpful because it points out statements which are to be specially noted and remembered and makes a useful distinction between basic and supplementary information. The reader must evaluate the material from his own point of view in order to select key words or sentences to underline. He may underline questionable statements, phrases not understood, sentences to be referred to later on, or even entire passages for review. Excessive underlining, however, tends to destroy the value of this technique by making no distinction between the most important and the less important ideas of the text. If you decide to underline selected passages, do so sparingly, with discretion. You may wish also to write in the margins brief queries or comments about the underlined passages. If you share a book with other readers, they will see and perhaps benefit from your underlining and notations.

Proper underlining can sometimes save time when you wish to recall ideas or episodes in a book after a long interval but find it inconvenient or tedious to reread the entire volume. If you have underlined properly during your original reading, you will be able to glance through the underlined sentences, reviewing the main points, and select immediately those passages you wish to reread carefully. You can experience once more the same pleasure that you felt during the first reading, even to a greater degree because you will not have to reread uninteresting or trivial parts of the book.

Students may use a double line to underline the most significant points in a textbook and list the double-lined pages on the inside front cover of their textbook. This technique makes it easy to find the key passages or ideas of an entire book quickly at a future time.

Copying. In view of the current emphasis on speed in reading, it may seem strange to advocate copying as one of the most valuable aids to reading efficiency. In order to copy specific sentences or passages, you must concentrate on the meaning of each sentence or passage and evaluate it before deciding whether or not it is worth copying. Moreover, when you copy anything you are compelled to read slowly and carefully and to think about the author's ideas and their relationship to his preceding ideas. Copying corrects the bad habit of careless skimming over any material which needs to be read slowly and carefully. Try this technique by reading a long letter or document quickly and then setting it aside for an hour or two before copying it. Usually you will notice new information or new implications in the material, things not readily appreciated in a rapid, cursory first reading. You may, for example, read a letter or contract from beginning to end and conclude that everything in it is simple and clear, only to discover that writing a copy reveals omissions, obscurities, or important new points to consider. Therefore, if you wish to make certain that you understand a significant passage thoroughly, take the time to copy it.

Reviewing and Self-Testing. Methods of reviewing and self-testing have frequently been used by students preparing for examinations or advanced study of a subject. Similar procedures are useful for a reader who wishes to remember the information he has read and to derive more benefit from his reading. It is best to review immediately after reading a chapter, article, or book, and thereafter at intervals. If you have written a summary or outline of the material, try at first to recall the details from memory and then compare your mental review with the written résumé. This procedure is especially valuable in preventing you from recalling only a partial or mistaken interpretation of the author's ideas. Too often a reader forgets exceptions or qualifications in the original text and remembers isolated statements out of context as if they were entirely true or adequate. Reviewing with a good outline prevents incorrect assumptions of this kind. It is sometimes better to forget all about an author's ideas than to form a distorted or mistaken view of them. Always check your review carefully against summaries, outlines, or the original work.

Self-testing is an excellent way to review a chapter or section of a book. You may sometimes test yourself by thinking of questions and answers, but it is usually best to write them down. Then consult the original text to check up on any significant points about which you failed to ask questions and to verify your answers. Keep your final list of questions and answers in a notebook so that you will be able to go back to them at intervals to refresh your memory and to insert your new interpretations and reactions.

Another splendid way to review is to explain the author's views to or discuss his main points with other people. Tell them what you think of his ideas and style of writing and ask for their opinions. When you try to teach what you have learned to others, you may sometimes discover that your knowledge is not so nearly perfect as you had assumed it to be, and you will then be able to improve your own understanding of the topic. Above all, hasten to correct your mistakes or prejudiced opinions, because delay may make it difficult or even impossible to correct them.

In short, remember that too many readers postpone careful rereading and then become occupied with other matters, remaining saddled for years to come with distorted or absurd misinterpretations of articles or books they have read. By testing your knowledge about a subject before and after rereading, you can improve your understanding of the subject and discuss it more intelligently with others. But what you do with ideas and information you read will provide the final test of your reading achievements. Experience is the best kind of test.

SELECTING TIME FOR READING

What is the best time for reading? The answer is, Whenever you can put enough time and attention into it to get something worthwhile out of it. You will get much out of your reading if you remember the author's central ideas and most effective passages. Psychologists claim that you will remember these best if you take a complete rest or even sleep after reading a while. The theory is that there will then be very few, if any, conflicting thoughts to interfere with or block out what you have read.

It seems logical to assume that if you read for hours at a time without a stop, hundreds of ideas may so overcrowd your mind that they may prevent concentration upon any of them. If there are too many things to remember, you will tend to forget them all. A rest period will often prevent such overcrowding, clearing the way for later recall of at least a few definite ideas. If you do not rest but continue reading, at least change to another kind of reading material—from rigid or technical matter to popular texts, from serious discussions to humor or light reading, or from history to fiction or poetry. Best of all, after reading an hour or two, take a walk, listen to music, talk with your friends, or follow up some other personal interests. Then go back to your reading with a fresh outlook and renewed vigor. You will enjoy it more and remember it well.

PREPARING TO READ

Most people read to the best advantage in a quiet, well-lighted place, seated in a comfortable but not too comfortable chair, with a dictionary, other reference works, pen, and notepaper handy; others do not mind noise or various distractions and perhaps like to read while listening to music; and some readers like to read leisurely in bed. It is said that Samuel Johnson, during periods of illness, cut holes in his bedsheet so that he could put his hands through them to hold a book which he could read while remaining snug and warm in bed. Abe Lincoln did much of his boyhood reading while stretched out on the floor. Children read all sorts of books in all sorts of places and positions.

There are some well-established practical suggestions about preparing to read. When you expect to read for any extended period, select a firm chair, keep your posture straight without excessive strain, hold the book or magazine in both hands at a distance permitting clear vision with both eyes and with a glare-free light—neither too bright nor too dim—coming either over your left shoulder or from any direction provided that it does not throw a shadow on the page or shine directly into your eyes. Keep your reference works, pen, paper, and clock nearby. If your thoughts stray occasionally while reading, be sure to avoid noise or distractions of any kind and you will find that absolute quiet will help you to concentrate. Some readers like to read with background music, despite the distractions; in most cases they will be disturbed much more by vocal selections than by instrumental (orchestral or chamber) music. In short, plan for the best possible conditions and get into the proper mood for earnest effort if you wish to derive the most benefit from your reading.

Do you often read in bed, either when indisposed or when you retire at night and try to read yourself to sleep? Some poor sleepers read a dull treatise or unexciting story instead of using medication to counteract their insomnia. A good suggestion is to read only a small but complete unit or separable portion of an interesting magazine or book, because you can finish reading that part or at least its main ideas before putting out the light. Make up your mind not to read beyond a certain page or chapter. Set your deadline and hold to it, remembering that tomorrow evening will be another evening for reading.

Some people who ordinarily neglect their reading will occasionally decide to read a large volume or several volumes for hours on end without rest periods. It is far better to plan your reading in accordance with a regular schedule, thus avoiding the danger of eyestrain and damage to health or other personal interests. You will enjoy your reading material more and get more out of it if you divide it into logically separable parts and finish only one or two at a time. In reading, as in most other pursuits, moderation and regularity are usually conducive to the best results.

USING BOOKS MOST EFFECTIVELY

Books contain certain special features, too frequently ignored, which readers can use to good advantage. These include copyright pages, tables of contents, prefaces, and introductions.

Examine the copyright page carefully, noting when the book was first published and whether or not there has been a revised or new edition or a new printing. There can be considerable difference between the copyright and printing dates—it is the copyright date which tells whether the book is a recently created work. Do not be misled by printing dates into assuming that an old book has been brought up to date or that a book with a recent printing date is a new publication. Read the preface without fail, for it may give information about the history of the author's work on the book—why he wrote it, the best way to use it, and what you can expect to get out of it. The table of contents, besides listing the chapter titles and sometimes a good deal more, also shows the arrangement and relationship of the various topics. Finally, if there is an introduction, it is likely to be a significant and useful part of the front matter. An introduction can explain the author's point of view, provide background information about the subject matter, or preview the principal themes of the book. Looking through the front matter of several books may help you to decide which ones to read. For this purpose, one alert reader who prefers light reading at bedtime reads the preface, then leafs through the book quickly to see how much dialogue is included, because complex discussions and descriptions would require serious concentration.

3

How To Remember
What You Read

What is memory? Is it only a shadow of the past? One of the most influential theories, at least two thousand four hundred years old, states that memory depends upon, and consists mainly of, associations among ideas. Plato pointed out in his *Phaedo* that seeing an object may immediately remind us of its owner. It is certainly true that events which go together or occur in close proximity tend to be linked together again in memory. Often when we see two things at the same time we connect them so that we can later think about either of them if the other reappears. The theory of association between ideas has been one of the foundations for modern psychologies of learning. Thus, Pavlov's system of conditioning was based on experiments proving that if an animal repeatedly links two things in sequence, subsequent awareness of one will impel him to recall and react to the other. Freud's system of psychoanalysis is based in part on his discovery that some ideas associated with unpleasant experiences are buried deep in our "unconscious minds" and must be brought to the surface (recalled) in order to cure a neurosis.

As a matter of fact, occasionally we remember things without apparent associations or perhaps with extremely remote associations. Freud's "unconscious," too, does not satisfy us completely as a theory, for we can sometimes submerge or repress painful experiences yet later recall them more vividly than the pleasant ones—all without nervous tension, neurosis, or psychiatric help.

One interesting theory compares memory to the action of electric waves creating pathways or patterns in the nervous system. According to this theory, such waves or currents produce new pathways, some more definite and effective or energetic than others, and new experiences engender additional waves which spread throughout the nervous system until they find and fit into the same pathways as before. An exciting experience is remembered better because its wave currents make deep pathways into which new thoughts fit as memories. The experience of recall not only thus produces an imitation of the original exciting event but also creates energy currents and pathways of its own so that we can later remember that we have remembered the original.

A PRACTICAL VIEW OF MEMORY

The association of ideas has practical value. If you associate a new idea which you have just read with old ones, your subsequent recollection of the old ideas may remind you of the new one. Unfortunately, you may too frequently be unable to recall the old ideas either, making these associations impossible. But this shortcoming of association can to some extent be counteracted by another related factor, namely, repetition. Information that has been repeated often enough with understanding will make a lasting impression and will be recallable later when you need it. But casual repetition of the ideas you read is not sufficient; to remember well, you must also pay attention to the meaning and order (organization) of the words and sentences. Since meaning and order depend upon association of ideas, both repetition and association are usually necessary.

Psychologists today divide memory into three parts: retention (we retain past experience in our mental storehouse for possible recall, never completely forgetting anything); recall (we recollect or think again about some of the stored experiences); and recognition (we recognize things because something about them reminds us of their identity and the fact that we have previously known them). Such an analysis corresponds to our common-sense practical interpretation.

In popular usage, retention refers to all the experiences which we can recall. If we cannot recall something that has happened, we say that we have failed to retain it, that we have forgotten it, and we are surprised if we suddenly remember it at a later time. The original thought or feeling has of course come and gone, but we can think about it again. Thus, memory is spoken of as if it meant the rediscovery of things we had stored away, from which we may eventually select one or more at our will and pleasure.

According to Freud, all ideas and other experiences are still with us, in the storehouse of our minds, including the forgotten ones which are either latent, or repressed in our unconscious (the repressed ones being the unpleasant experiences). He pointed out that thinking and talking about past experiences may help us to recall the repressed ones, recognize them for what they are, and begin to understand why we repressed them, thus relieving nervous tension.

Actually, science knows little that can be proved about the unconscious, the subconscious, or any other fundamental aspect of memory. Many people agree with Freud that the repression of unpleasant childhood experiences can lead to psychological disturbances in adult years. But there is no scientific proof of the existence of an unconscious realm, a subterranean vault in the nervous system; the psychological disturbances of an adult may be due to a feeling of inadequacy—not to repressed memories of his childhood experiences, but simply to a realization that he has been unable to understand or cope with unpleasant conditions (the details of which he has "forgotten")— or to conflicting choices whether to think about or ignore painful incidents. He becomes tense because he does not know how to deal with serious problems, which road to take. A person who keeps thinking about shocking incidents of his early childhood, without feelings of inadequacy or despair, may easily recall the details at a later time and usually without excessive tension or the development of a neurosis. At any rate, for reading improvement, we are here concerned only with practical methods of facilitating recall.

EFFECTIVE WAYS TO RECALL

Among the most effective, practical ways to facilitate recall of reading materials are the following: enthusiastic interest; intention to recall; evaluation; concentration; repetition; application; and organization.

Enthusiastic Interest. If we read a number of passages casually, we may retain them all somewhere in memory but each will be difficult to recall because it will be only one of many comparable units. If we want to recall a particular passage or idea, what will make us think again about that one instead of the others? If we paid special attention to it, the one we later want to remember would have made a stronger impression than the others and would therefore be likely to reappear in our thoughts. But why do we pay special attention to some things instead of others? Usually because they can help us in some way or because they are related to our vital interests and needs. Therefore, one of the best ways to strengthen the impression made by the ideas we want to remember is to connect them with something else that is familiar and important to us.

For example, I had read about a state law affecting property rights but had given it little attention and forgot its provisions. But when I became involved in litigation wherein the same law could seriously affect my property, I reread the law, this time with special interest and attention. Thereafter I could never again forget the provisions of that law. It had become significant reading material worth recalling because I saw its relationship to something about which I was deeply concerned. When you read something you want to remember, try to connect it with as many real interests as possible so that it will long remain near the surface of your memory for instant recall and use. Ask yourself, *How will this infor-*

mation affect me or my associates and why should I try to remember it? The question itself will tend to stimulate your interest and thus greatly increase the likelihood of recall.

Intention to Recall. Much reading material consists of relatively minor points built around or contributing to the main ideas. You will forget such details, but when you come to a significant idea, stop and think of it as something you will want to remember, then reread it slowly and deliberately. You must not only understand and repeat the idea but you must also label it as one worth remembering, that is to say, as one you are determined to recollect at the proper time. (If you have not fully understood the idea, you may remember only the fact that you have failed to understand it, for there will be no clear meaning in your mind to retain. There will be nothing to recall.)

It is sometimes difficult to decide what to reread with intention to recall. Usually the topic sentences or other key sentences are the ones you will select for this purpose. You may also choose key paragraphs to emphasize in the same way. Further, even though the main ideas in the original version are perfectly clear to you when you read them, restate them in your own words, in the habitual vocabulary that you will want to use when you hopefully will recall them. Now they will fit perfectly into the orderly system of those things you are determined to remember. You will be able to concentrate on the ideas themselves as you would express them, without interference from the unfamiliar language of a stranger.

With rare exceptions, it is a mistake to try to read everything with intention to recall. There is a limit to the number of things you can or should commit to memory for recollection, and the effectiveness of the method depends upon discrimination between what is worth the effort and what should be forgotten. Some people read everything too casually, soon forgetting all of it, while others read and reread every sentence too diligently and after the ordeal is over they, too, forget everything. Both types of readers should change their habits and become selective, discriminating, and more alert to the things worth rereading with intention to recall.

Make sure that you correctly interpret what you reread and express it correctly in your own words, for a mistaken interpretation may persist in your memory and may then be extremely difficult to eradicate. Too often people read and reread carelessly and thus fix the errors firmly in their memories so that they recall and repeat the mistakes ad infinitum.

You may wish to test your ability to recall things you have read with intention to recall. For this purpose note the picture on page 47. Examine the picture carefully and as you read the list of forty objects on this page, find in the picture each of the objects listed. Then take a blank sheet of paper and, without looking at the printed list below or at the picture, write down the names of all the objects you can remember. Next compare your written list with the printed one. If you have recalled most of the forty objects listed, you have a superior ability to recall things which you read with intention to recall.

1. andirons (in fireplace)
2. ashtray (on mantel)
3. ball (in dog's mouth)
4. bottle (on table)
5. boy
6. chair
7. cord (window shade pull)
8. cup
9. dog
10. doily (on table)
11. doll
12. drape (or curtain)
13. electric fixture (on wall)
14. electric light bulbs
15. electric outlet
16. electric plug
17. fireplace
18. flowers (in vase)
19. girl
20. gun
21. knife
22. lamp
23. log
24. mantel
25. mirror
26. picture (shown in mirror)
27. pipe (in ashtray)
28. plate
29. radiator
30. saucer
31. skate
32. spoon
33. straw (in bottle)
34. table
35. teddy bear
36. tray (on table)
37. tricycle
38. vase
39. window
40. window shade (or blind)

Evaluation. I once read a poorly written newspaper column several times, but it left me puzzled and disappointed. I have forgotten the details in that column, but I do remember that the writing was badly organized and ambiguous. Why did I forget the information itself, yet recall easily the poor quality of the writing? Because I had especially noticed and evaluated the inept writing which distracted my attention from the ideas being presented. If I had been able to concentrate on and react to the ideas themselves, they, too, would probably have persisted in my memory. Similarly, in your reading, you will usually remember best the things that impress you sufficiently so that you evaluate or otherwise react to them.

Even in our everyday casual reading, and certainly in our more serious-minded reading, we make distinctions between major and minor ideas. Surely it is impractical to try to recall everything we read, for that, if it could be done, would overload our minds with trivial or useless information. Evaluate carefully what is most meaningful and significant in your reading, and then you will have a good chance to recall these relatively few things when you have need of them. If you read a paragraph and can then say to yourself, *This is an important idea worth remembering,* you will indeed be most likely to remember it well. Such an evaluation involves repetition: first, you think about the meaning of the idea and, second, you think again about the idea when you ascribe great importance to it. But do not make the mistake of exaggerating the significance of so many ideas that the distinction between their values becomes confused. Try to make certain that the main points you select are really the ones that will be most worth recalling.

During the past thirty years or more I have had occasion to read, reread, and edit hundreds of books in various subjects and today remember best those ideas and presentations which I believed to be either unusually good or extremely dubious. I have forgotten most of the detailed information, but can recall those major points which I evaluated. In a sense, all readers should function as book editors to the best of their ability, judging which statements are true or partly true, logical or absurd, clearly set forth or confusing. Sometimes the reading material which is difficult to understand is worth studying until the reader can estimate its truth and importance, because serious study involving a concentrated search for meanings may insure permanent retention and ready recall. You may easily forget what is handed to you ready-made, but you will long remember what you look hard for and find for yourself.

One of the best ways to evaluate reading material, a way often used by experienced book editors, is that of comparison and contrast. An editor compares important ideas and discussions in one book with those in other books, noting in which respects they agree, in which they disagree, and which manner of expression is clearest and best organized. Any reader can make excellent use of this technique. As you read, think back to your past reading of similar topics and compare the present material with it. How do the new ideas differ from the old? Which do you prefer, and which would be most worth keeping in mind for subsequent reference? Are the new ideas true to your life experience? Just as nations can and should (but seldom do) learn from comparisons between present situations and those of the past—from the lessons of history—so you as an individual should learn and well remember present reading by comparing it with your past reading experiences. Sometimes, too, you can compare the same author's ideas with those in other books he has written, noting similarities and differences which you will later easily recall. You may even find inconsistencies in different parts of a single article or book. Note also the manner in which one part supplements or reinforces the others. Analysis of this kind greatly increases the likelihood of recall.

Finally, you should evaluate the reading material as a whole experience. Ask yourself, Did I really enjoy this author's work? If you think about the reasons for your reactions, you will perhaps review some of the highlights of the material and fix them more firmly in your memory. Notice especially any unexpected, disturbing, or unfinished points. If you evaluate the author's work with either favorable or unfavorable criticisms, the special attention you thus bestow upon it will be compensated by more effective retention and recall.

Concentration. Every reader has had the experience of trying to read while distracted by other matters, such as personal problems or annoying interruptions. Efficiency in reading requires concentration upon the author's meaning. If the reader cannot grasp the meaning of what he has read, there will be nothing significant in his mind for him to remember. Concentration means searching for ideas while excluding distractions; it means shutting out irrelevant thoughts in order to follow the trend of the author's words. When your attentive efforts result in understanding, you will tend to remember your achievement—the meanings you have discovered— for most people remember their achievements and forget their failures. Shut out all unrelated thoughts and preoccupations, give your wholehearted attention to the author's main ideas, and you will be likely to understand and remember them.

Often the ability to concentrate depends upon self-interest. If you are reading something which is of no concern to you, which does not affect you, which fails to evoke your sympathy or antipathy, it is quite certain that you will be looking at the words without earnest attention and will quickly forget them. For example, a housewife who is intensely interested in cooking will read recipes with close attention, promptly noticing anything new or particularly useful in them. Someone else, even though skilled in reading, may find the same recipes quite boring, may read them with scant attention, and may impatiently discard and forget them. Thus, to insure serious concentration, you must connect reading material with your favorite interests—your own ideas, experiences, opinions, conversations, associations, and activities.

If you have begun reading without close attention, stop and ask yourself, *Why am I reading this*? If you cannot think of a satisfactory reason, put your reading aside. If you decide that the material is worthwhile, begin again, this time with enough effort to insure close attention and full comprehension. Inattentive reading is careless reading, hasty, superficial, seldom worth the attempt. Anything worth reading at all should be read with attention and concentration.

How much should you try to concentrate on reading at a single sitting? Obviously, if you keep staring at a paragraph and repeating the words, you will soon lose interest and get nowhere. To concentrate, the mind must be active; it must think about one logical point after another or it will go blank. The amount of material you can read efficiently at one sitting will vary with the time available, the difficulty of the text, and your ability to concentrate on it.

Some readers cannot keep their attention steady on a line of thought for five minutes at a time, but wander off, filling their minds with trivial information which crowds out the author's important ideas. Other readers can read on and on for hours without giving more attention to one point than to another. If you wish to improve recall, avoid both extremes. Divide the material into just the right amount of solid intellectual food you can comfortably digest, think about it in a logical way as you read, then pause and let it sink in. When you resume reading, notice the links among the parts and you will have the best chance to remember the whole passage.

The middle parts of a reading selection are usually more difficult to remember than the beginning and end parts. Therefore, before you read each new section, it may be helpful to skim through the preceding sections again, giving special attention to the middle part and linking its ideas to the rest. A novel, for example, can often be subdivided into logical parts based on the plot. Some readers can remember an unfinished story better than a completed one. If you divide a novel into its natural parts and read several with sustained interest, you will be kept in suspense and will remember well the unresolved events. Such unfinished episodes of novels serialized in newspapers and magazines used to attract many readers who could hardly wait to buy the next issue—proving that reading in parts of reasonable length sustains interest and recall.

Repetition. Repetition is a most potent factor in the recall of reading material. It may be partial or complete, direct or indirect, attentive and meaningful or inattentive and casual. Reading materials may be repeated in the same sequence or their order may be modified or even reversed. Moreover, repeated readings can never be exactly the same, because each repetition affects the power of the reader to understand and complete the next rereading, especially since he has now become more alert to what lies ahead of him. Thus, if you read a paragraph once, you may get a general idea of its message; when you read it again, you will find it easier to read quickly and may also notice additional ideas or implications in it. We think with the thoughts we have had in the past.

You do not always have to reread every word. If you are reading a complicated mass of information, try rereading only the main points several times, keeping your mind from being overcrowded or confused by too many details at one time. You may decide to skim over some parts which seem to contribute little to the author's message and to reread the essentials more carefully than before. Often, instead of rereading the original sentences directly from the printed source, you may do better to review them indirectly by rethinking the ideas in your mind. In some cases, you may wish to skip a paragraph here and there, or reverse the sequence, rereading a later part before an earlier one. (But do not lose track of the author's logical arrangement of his ideas.) All these forms of repetition can improve the ability to recall.

Psychological experiments have shown that repetitions

are more effective if they are spread over several periods of time instead of being concentrated into one period. For example, assume that to remember a few selected passages or events you plan to reread them, say, ten times each. You will recall them much better if you read them five times on each of two days than you will if you read them ten times in a single day.

Why does a moderate delay in repetitions help recall? One explanation states that each group of repetitions makes impressions on the mind which grow stronger for a while thereafter; consequently, a waiting period after each set of repetitions allows the impressions to become still more firmly fixed in the memory. But there is doubt as to the validity of this explanation, for impressions usually grow weaker, not stronger, with the passing of time, during which new, interfering experiences crowd into the mind. A more plausible explanation might be that a second set of immediate repetitions are of less value than delayed ones because the reader remembers the first reading well enough, and repetitions add little to his interest or to what he already knows; in fact, he tends to reread hastily or casually. A day later, the reader will still remember part of the material, but he will need another set of attentive repetitions and will concentrate on them because he knows they will help him to recapture the whole story. The things he has forgotten since yesterday are the weak links which the new set of repetitions can emphasize and strengthen. (Athletes, public speakers, and musicians have always been aware of the special value of distributed practice.) Note, however, that if the reader waits too long before rereading, say, several weeks, he will probably have forgotten too much and will have to start all over again.

Early experiments on memory proved that the rate of forgetting is extremely rapid immediately after the first readings. Forgetting continues thereafter, but at a slower rate. For this reason, you should not wait too long before rereading or at least rethinking the materials you may later wish to recall. Unfortunately, many students preparing for examinations repeat a lesson many times in one day and remember enough to pass their examinations the next day, but they will eventually forget nearly everything. Cramming is a useless method of learning even though it enables students to pass examinations.

For practical purposes, when you have read certain ideas which you would like to remember permanently, review them several times in your mind every few days. Do not depend on numerous repetitions within one session only, for you have no immediate need of them, and too many of them can become frustrating and tedious— even though a limited amount of overlearning (unnecessary repetition) is unavoidable and sometimes helpful. On the other hand, do not let too much time elapse before rethinking the same ideas, because additional interfering experiences will blot out the original material. Repetitions must have something to build upon, some partial recall, to fill in gaps or serve as cues to refresh the memory.

Application. One of the best ways to improve recall of reading material is to apply it. Let me cite an example. I purchased an appliance consisting of two machines which had to be put together by means of a hitch. I read the manual of directions carefully, including instructions for assembling and for using the equipment. But when I began putting the two parts together, I could not recall the first steps. Later I could not remember how each step I did recall fitted into the others. So I reread only one sentence at a time and followed its directions meticulously. Now, as I applied what I had read and reread, I understood clearly and remembered easily what each of the directions meant. I soon came to the last sentence, a final step, instructing me to slide the second machine forward on top of the first and then to push a long handle forward. I did these things as directed, but the two parts simply would not remain hitched together. As soon as I pulled one, they separated. Obviously there was something wrong. I lay flat on the ground and, recalling the last sentence in the directions, watched to see what would happen when I pushed the long handle forward. I saw that the two parts to be fastened together did not even touch, so I continued to press forward very hard on the handle until a rod on the first machine pushed a spring down so that the two machines could be moved along until firmly joined together. I have never forgotten these directions because I applied them successfully to solve a real problem. Of course, the manual was at fault because, instead of merely instructing the reader to push the long handle forward, it should have told him to push it forward hard as far as it would go and it should have explained why that was necessary. I supplemented the printed instructions with my own information and the entire solution of the problem remained vividly in my mind thereafter.

Not all applications are so practical as that one. Some of the most useful ones take place in the reader's imagination. Others occur during conversations or other contacts with people. If you wish to strengthen your recall of the significant materials you read, use the ideas in a variety of ways—express them in your own words, discuss them, teach them, write about them, think them over, put them into practice, visualize them, draw pictures or diagrams of them, supplement them with ideas of your own. Such applications improve understanding and facilitate recall. Moreover, do not forget to distribute applications over several periods of time so that both the ideas and their uses will benefit from spaced repetition.

Nearly everything we learn involves the fitting together of old and new information. We apply past learnings to present ones. We think with our past, a reservoir of intellectual tools. There could be no mental experience of any significance without this kind of application. You have learned the meanings of certain words and when you apply the old meanings to new sentences which you are reading, you will usually remember the old ones better than before, and they will serve as foundations for understanding and remembering the new ones. For example, you may recall that *bon* means good in French. When you read the words *bon mot* in an English sentence, you will apply the meaning of *bon* to the word *mot* (meaning word), and thereafter you will recall that the two words together mean "good word," or "clever remark." Thus, application in your imagination, that is, your thinking about the associations between things, is an effective aid to memory. The vigorous interplay of ideas in your own mind can often become the swiftest and most useful pathway to better recall.

Organization. Man is the great systematizer, the organizer par excellence. He puts things together and tears them apart, rearranges them, turns them upside down and inside out, and ties them in neat bundles. Reading, or any kind of logical thinking, depends upon organization of parts within wholes. Not only the individual words or single ideas, but the combinations of them into sentences, paragraphs, and sections are presented as an organized set or system. If you notice and remember the organization as a whole, you will better remember each of its parts.

Reading and rereading a whole set of ideas at one time and rereading each part separately several times will help you to recall all of them. The psychologists call this method the learning of the whole and its parts. If the entire set of passages is not too long or complicated, the first reading provides an adequate framework into which you can fit the various parts. If you wish to remember a discussion, read the whole of it, then read each part several times, and, finally, reread the entire discussion, noting the way in which the parts are linked together.

The surprise element in a sequence or organized pattern of ideas is probably responsible for better recall of reading material. If everything you read were old and familiar to you, you would take it for granted and be inclined to forget it. The same surprise element is often the secret of humor. Consider, for example, the story about Abe Lincoln's journey through a rural community late at night. Abe stopped at the roadside to ask a farmer standing nearby whether he could put him and his horse up for the night. The farmer stared into the sky but made no answer. Finally, Abe rode off and found lodging elsewhere. The next evening he happened to be passing on the same road and there was the farmer, standing in the identical spot and still staring into the sky. As Abe reached him, the farmer nodded his head and gave him his answer, "Yes." The humor in this story depends on the surprise element in the sequence of events—the gap of twenty-four hours between question and answer and the unexpected twist in the idea that the farmer was still thinking about Abe's question. The story is supposed to show how slowly the rural people of his time reacted to emergencies.

When you read, reread, and rethink what you have read, you may omit the less important points, but take special notice of the surprises, difficulties, and unexpected features in the orderly sequence of ideas. Review the pattern of the author's material in your mind. Is it chronological? Are there causes leading to results? Do the main ideas consist of one or several themes or motifs, with supporting evidence or arguments? Does the author supply additional information as the basis for a significant conclusion? Does he approach a problem from several points of view? Does he go back and forth, repeat himself, jump around from one idea to another? If you have grasped the author's plan for a whole section, remembering one part will later remind you of the others. Moreover, since you will usually be able to recall the beginning and the end of the entire material, keeping the author's system in mind will help you to fill in the middle parts.

4
How To Analyze What You Read

The preceding discussion has reviewed ways to achieve satisfactory speed and comprehension in reading. The most important factors affecting retention and recall of reading materials were also considered. The discussion in this chapter and the next two chapters will deal with methods of reading which distinguish expert readers from merely average readers.

It is their ability in critical reading which characterizes the most alert and efficient readers. In one sense, reading proficiency can be compared with musical accomplishment. Thus, an amateur musician may acquire modest skill in the performance and appreciation of instrumental music, but much more is required of the professional musician. In the same way, readers can go far beyond the mastery of reading habits and methods which result in only average understanding and can become alert consumers of written communications of every kind. By learning and practicing the principles of critical reading to be discussed, you can develop some of the advanced skills of the truly expert readers, delving more deeply and carefully into each author's work. Furthermore, you will be less apt to become a victim of careless or unscrupulous writers interested chiefly in money-making or one-sided propaganda instead of intellectual service to mankind and the diffusion of knowledge through communication of the truth.

The writer's work reflects to some extent his own character and experience. (Rare indeed are the universal geniuses, such as Shakespeare, whose masterpieces fail to reveal much about the personal backgrounds of their authors.) At the same time, however, the meaning and power of the words presented by the writer depend upon the ability of the reader to interpret them. He gets out of them only what he himself puts into them. Obviously, to get the most out of his reading, he must devote adequate attention and thought to the material being read. Too many people derive little benefit from their reading because they fail to make sufficient preparation for it. They do not even resolve to be careful and critical, but simply plunge ahead from one paragraph to the next, often overwhelmed by what appear to be convincing facts or arguments. They interpret everything on the basis of previous untested opinions and assumptions, thus confirming their own prejudices and reinforcing their own mistakes. The expert reader, on the other hand, is well-versed in the logic of reading—in the rational principles of communication and the skills necessary for comprehension in depth.

THE LOGIC OF READING

The most useful principles of the logic of reading can be applied easily by any reader who will discipline himself to remember and make regular use of them. The basic principles are those of inclusiveness, reality, proportion, momentum, analogy, emphasis, and implication. Observation of these principles in practice will deepen and enrich the reading of newspapers, periodicals, and books.

Inclusiveness. In any kind of printed matter, serious omissions of relevant ideas or information, whether purposive or inadvertent, need to be detected and counteracted by the reader, because such omissions can greatly affect his understanding of the work. They impair the validity and quality of expression in fiction or nonfiction, news, prose, drama, or poetry. Consider, for example, the following paragraphs entitled *Flag-Waving, Flag-Burning,* and *Flag-Saving.*

Flag-Waving

This country enjoys the highest standard of living in the world. It has nearly half the world's telephones. It has four times as many automobiles as any other nation and 58 per cent of the total, produces more than twice as much electricity as any other country, nine times as many miles of airlines, three times as much aluminum, twice as much rubber, has the largest merchant fleet, leads the world in cement production, petroleum, lead, coal, copper, steel, zinc, cheese production, cotton, oats, and meat. With only 6 per cent of the world's population, we own about 50 per cent of its wealth. We lead the world, too, in education, literacy, life insurance, science and invention, home ownership, railroad mileage, radio and television sets. We enjoy free enterprise, free speech, free education, and the best health aids and medical facilities of any people in history. Moreover, we have sent to foreign countries 100 billion dollars to assist them in meeting their economic and social problems. We have never lost a war. We lead the world in space exploration. All these achievements have been made by our free people in a competitive, profit-making society which has proved itself to be superior to any other, past or present. It is no wonder that millions of people have come to us from all parts of the earth to escape enslavement, lack of opportunity, and oppression.

Everything in the preceding paragraph is consistent with the facts. If the reader merely accepts these statements without critical analysis, he will inevitably conclude that all is for the best in this best of all possible worlds—and he will be doing inestimable damage both to his own conscience and to the well-being of his country. The prospect of social progress becomes extremely dubious if citizens assume that perfection or near-perfection has already been attained. Any reader sincerely concerned about the welfare of his own community and nation should read such information in the light of life experience and the conflicting evidence offered by writers presenting a different view of the same subject. The following paragraph, *Flag-Burning,* contrasts sharply with the one above, and yet its information, too, is quite true and consistent with the facts.

Flag-Burning

This nation is afflicted by one of the highest crime rates in the world, with nearly three million major crimes reported in a single year and more than four million arrests. In many cities violence occurs so often that it has been unsafe to walk in the streets. Presidents and other leading citizens have been assassinated. Large-scale organizations of gangsters operate in all parts of the country, frequently with the connivance of official-dom. Family life is at a low level, with one in every four marriages ending in divorce. The strain and stress of our society are reflected by the fact that half a million patients are being treated in mental hospitals at any one time, and they are only a small part of the millions in need of therapy. We own more automobiles than any other country and drive them farther, but at a price of 55,000 deaths each year in automobile accidents—one death every eleven minutes day and night—and millions of accidents, partly due to chronic alcoholism among drivers, disregard of others, and unsafe cars distributed by corporations which must earn profits for stockholders by manufacturing, advertising, and marketing over-sized, superficially pleasing but flimsy and dangerous over-powered and frequently defective vehicles. We are the world's largest producers and consumers of tobacco, which has caused millions to die prematurely and pain-fully from heart disease, lung cancer, and other ailments. Yet, those who manufacture or advertise such deadly products as tobacco earn handsome profits and become respected pillars of the community. They persuade peo-ple to use more of their toxic products and then they boast that they are merely giving them what they want. Six million of our people are confirmed alcoholics. The very air, waters, and forests of our land are con-stantly being polluted for the temporary benefit of the money-makers. We send our youth off to wars resulting in millions of casualties in order to protect financial in-terests and national power and prestige throughout the world. Everywhere we find instances of deception, chicanery, rationalization, flag-waving, schemes to ac-quire wealth, and deceitful advertising, business mo-nopoly, labor racketeering, corruption even in the arts and professions. The social climate remains muddied by racial and religious hatred and bigotry and class antag-onisms.

Obviously, this second paragraph is just as one-sided as the first, and just as dangerous. Both comments suffer from omissions, from disregard of the principle of inclusiveness. The alert reader will find each of them unconvincing. The next paragraph, entitled *Flag-Saving,* suggests the method whereby readers can fill in the omissions of ideas in reading material to achieve accurate and balanced understanding of a subject.

Flag-Saving

Our country, though beset with serious problems and difficulties, has numerous achievements to its credit. We have made mistakes, tragic ones, yet it has been better to face our problems boldly than to do nothing about them, for inaction is the greatest mistake of all. Standards of living are comparatively high, but we must admit that the price being paid by the people is also high. If we lead in transportation, we also lead in accidents; if we enjoy a high level of education, too much of the effort is superficial, wasteful, and ineffective. We should balance the good in our society against the evil—blinding ourselves to either will only conceal the truth necessary for the enlargement of our freedoms and the improvement of our condition. We have indeed failed to prevent disastrous trends in domestic affairs and have become embroiled in violence abroad, yet we have been prime movers in efforts to prevent further catastrophes and to build a world of peace, justice, and order.

Disregard of the principle of inclusiveness affects all forms of reading material. The skilled novelist or playwright develops his characters to make them seem really true to life and therefore genuine, interesting personalities. The unskilled novelist or playwright portrays wooden people or distorted characters with an ineptness that ruins his work. Perhaps the most serious defect in modern news-reporting and advertising is this lack of adequate information. Readers should discover this defect and reject such materials as a rational basis for reactions and decisions.

If you demand inclusiveness, you will eventually get it.

I recall that when I was a businessman in Boston, one of my customers was a famous old retail store, Raymond's "Where U Bot the Hat," a prosperous enterprise which owed much of its success to absolute honesty in its advertising and dealings with suppliers and patrons. If there was anything not quite perfect about its merchandise, Raymond's considered it a duty to so inform the public. People liked to trade in that store because it could be trusted never to conceal the truth. There are laws prohibiting fraudulent claims by merchants, but often appeal to the law is more costly than the damage caused to the individual—and there are few laws against silence. It has become common practice to tell people only what is good about a product or service, yet is this not just as deceitful as an outright falsehood? Indeed, far worse, for readers can sometimes investigate and reject a false statement but they are seldom expert enough to fill in the information which has been deliberately omitted. A small step has been taken to protect the public through laws regulating the purchase of insurance, stocks and bonds, and a few other products. But the best means of protection are twofold: an honorable business community, and truly alert consumers of information determined to deal only with those merchants and community leaders who can be trusted to "tell the truth, the whole truth."

Reality. The principle of reality, as applied to reading materials, refers to the degree of agreement between an author's works and the experience of the reader. When reading novels, even those featuring mythical, miraculous, or imaginary situations and events of the strangest kind, the expert reader measures the presentation against the yardstick of his life experience. The good and evil characters in literature are illumined through the recollection of events, dreams, and visions of living human beings. Even God is envisioned by pious men as all-wise, all-knowing, all-merciful, and the like—the familiar human qualities known to us all but now extrapolated to the highest level. The expert reader analyzes an author's work to ascertain in what ways it is true to life itself—how it is either similar to life experience or contrasted with life experience.

A modern reader generally does not believe in witches. Yet, when witches are encountered in masterpieces of literature, the reader forgets his cynicism and skepticism, allowing his imagination to roam freely in the author's fantastic world and seeking out the special qualities, powers, and activities of mythical beings *as if* he believed in them—*as if* they were true to life, and indeed they must be so in some way in order to be understood.

Thus, note the following passage from *Hamlet*, spoken by Hamlet as he takes the skull of the former King's jester Yorick from the grave. Hamlet muses that his wicked mother, the Queen, will, like the dead jester, some day die and turn into dust—so what good will her evil deeds do her then?

> Alas, poor Yorick! I knew him, Horatio: a fellow of infinite jest, of most excellent fancy: he hath borne me on his back a thousand times; and now, how abhorred in my imagination it is! my gorge rises at it. Here hung those lips that I have kissed I know not how oft. Where be your gibes now? your gambols? your songs? your flashes of merriment, that were wont to set the table on a roar? * Not one now, to mock your own grinning? Quite chap-fallen? ** Now get you to my lady's chamber, and tell her, let her paint an inch thick, to this favour she must come; make her laugh at that. . . .
> (*Hamlet*, Act V, Scene 1)

The alert reader of this magnificent passage must recall the jolly people who made merry in his childhood years, now dead and gone—the jolly people who, like Yorick, were so clever, gifted, playful—who have now, as all men, become lifeless bones, skulls that cannot grin or jest or

---

* The jesters told their jokes to the guests at the dinner table and they would roar with laughter.

** A word such as "chap-fallen" puzzles the modern reader or playgoer (it meant loss of the lower jaw as in the skull) but even here the sense is lifelike and carries the implication of coming to a bad end.

frolic again; so, too, will the clever Queen, the vain creature who paints her cheeks thickly, be unable to avoid the same fate; and if she realizes this, perhaps she will not be quite so lighthearted about her dishonor. Notice especially the repetition of reality in the repeated reminders that the dead jester had done so many happy things, yet now is but a horrible, detestable thing of dust —a fate shared by all mankind.

This passage was written by Shakespeare more than 350 years ago, but the reader can understand its universal meanings as he compares them with his own life experiences. As the noted Shakespearean scholar George Lyman Kittredge often reminded his students, Hamlet was not an artificially created type or formula but an individual caught up in the tragedy of his group, the royal house. Hamlet was a man of utmost sensitivity, like people we have all known, and we understand his words as the natural self-expression of such an individual in his life situation. True, not all readers will interpret his character precisely alike, but if they think critically as they read, they will see him as he would be in reality.

The principle of reality permeates social literature in writings and ideas of idealists such as Thomas Paine, Abraham Lincoln, and Ralph Waldo Emerson, in the works of novelists such as Theodore Dreiser, and of reformers such as Henry George. The reader must compare their sentiments with his own background of experience before he can fully appreciate the significance of the truths in their writings. Consider, for example, a few of the statements of these men:

> Thomas Paine—"The contrast between affluence and wretchedness is like dead and living bodies chained together." (Works, III, 337)
> Abraham Lincoln—"We don't propose any war on capital, we do wish to allow the humblest man an equal chance to get rich with anybody else . . ." (New Haven speech)
> Ralph Waldo Emerson—"The highest end of government is the culture of men, not the protection of property rights." (*Essay on Politics*)

Theodore Dreiser, expressing the philosophy of a character in *The Financier*—"It is a grim, bitter world we are all born into . . . who was to straighten out the matter of unjust equipment with which most people began?"

Henry George—advocating "a rearrangement of the industrial and social system on a higher ethical basis."

When you read and interpret ideas such as these, measure their validity against your own life experience with the people and institutions of your community. We expect authors of fiction to intermingle the real with the fantastic, what exists with the things they dream about, attempting to dress the mixture of fact, illusion, and fantasy with language most appropriate in mood and tone. But even the most imaginative of them put living people into their works—and the most gifted of them have sometimes been sued for portraying persons so realistically as to make them recognizable. On the other hand, too many works of literature are weakened by inclusion of lifeless or unrealistic character portraits. A humorous anecdote circulating in publishers' offices tells about a prospective author who attached a note to his manuscript stating that "the characters in my novel are not real persons and bear no resemblance to any persons living or dead." The publisher's rejection slip contained the brief comment: "That is precisely what is wrong with this manuscript." It is the principle of reality that gives strength and meaning to an author's works, and the expert reader goes back to life itself as a basis for understanding them in depth.

Proportion. Closely related to the principle of reality is that of proportion, which refers to the twofold process of exaggeration and understatement. These qualities in reading material are like magnifying and reducing mirrors held up to the realities of life. The reader must cope with exaggeration and understatement if he wishes to understand the true significance of many ideas.

Exaggeration magnifies reality and attracts the reader's attention to a stated or implied truth. Thus, Cervantes, the author of the powerful novel of the seventeenth century, *Don Quixote,* was enabled to exaggerate reality by making his hero a man driven insane from reading the chivalric tales then universally popular. Those tales relating the exploits of noble knights performing brave deeds are duplicated by Don Quixote as he converts his bony nag into an imaginary handsome charger, the flat-nosed, plain farm girl into a beautiful princess, and a paunchy farmer into his aristocratic squire. All sorts of exaggerated, impossible deeds are thereafter described in a most effective, humorous style by contrasting the theoretical ideals of chivalric literature with the totally contradictory, crushing, sordid realities of the times. The moral implications of this novel paved the way for a new attitude in literature and society—believe what you can see and feel, the world as it is, not the fanciful, never-existing world of your dreams.

Exaggeration is highly effective in stimulating or sharpening the impact of an author's ideas. I recall reading Heinrich Heine's observations about the town of Göttingen when he was leaving the university there after some bitter experiences. He commented that he had admired the beautiful limbs of the Göttingen ladies and had even thought that he might draw pictures of their legs— if he could find paper large enough for that purpose. Exaggeration is more often not quite so direct and pointed, but more indirect and subtle.

The principle of proportion suggests that you should evaluate the extent of exaggeration in reading materials and balance it with its opposite, understatement. The truth will usually lie somewhere between the two extremes. If all horses are noble champions and Don Quixote's nag Rocinante is a horse, then Rocinante is a noble champion despite her old age and bare bones— until you believe the evidence of your own eyes and hands when you see and touch her. You can admire the stubborn hero as he breaks his own ribs in fantastic adventures, and then appreciate fully the disillusionment he suffers when he comes to his senses and realizes the contrast between his visionary world of miracles and the world of evils, follies, injustice, the world as it is. Always, then, the exaggeration in great literature can be traced to the world of reality which it exaggerates. The reader must himself put the author's words and ideas into perspective, into correct proportions, and thus enrich his own understanding of the reading material.

Exaggeration and understatement are legitimate tools and techniques of the news reporter, novelist, essayist, playwright, and poet. There is no news in the millions of normal, everyday activities of people; there is news in murder, conflict, fire, catastrophe, the serious problems and difficulties of individual or community. The author selects one aspect of life to portray in his work and necessarily magnifies it while understating competing aspects. If he describes the condition of the poor, he must usually minimize the charities of the rich, for the reader's attention must not be too greatly distributed but must be concentrated upon the main theme. If, on the other hand, he selects aristocrats of a society for his central characters, he cannot portray fully all the customs and problems of the masses. It is your responsibility as an alert reader to put the contents of news reports, novels, plays, poems, into proper balance and proportion. In portraying the evils of slavery, Harriet Beecher Stowe was quite justified in selecting illustrations of cruelty and injustice; in depicting the evils of child labor and the economic system of his time, Charles Dickens did well to emphasize the despicable conditions of the poor and the grasping motives of the wealthy; in describing the evils of tyranny, war, and corruption, creative writers such as Ibsen, Tolstoy, and Upton Sinclair made those aspects of life the principal themes of their works. Few readers read enough to gain a balanced view of life and society from news or literature alone—they must sympathize, understand, but take into account exaggeration and understatement, the principle of proportion.

Momentum. Just as water in a stream flows on and on, so ideas in a novel or discussion seem to possess a forward impulse or momentum of their own. An unscrupulous or careless author gives his readers some facts in sequence, together with partial truths which they tend to accept and which precede untrue ideas tacked on at the end. Truth can easily carry falsehood along with it in the reader's mind. Conversely ideas which seem quite dubious may be rejected by a reader who later cannot accept the truth because he has lost confidence in the author's judgment. The main momentum comes from the accumulation of small ideas which induce the reader to accept larger conclusions or a point of view. Plausible opinions become the foundation of doubtful generalizations. Sometimes the conclusions may be correct and appropriate, but the reader should not assume this to be so. He should weigh and consider, never merely accepting submissively or uncritically the intellectual menu of subtle, one-sided, or superficial reading materials.

Beware of accepting so much of what you read that you begin to worship the printed word, the authority, in essays, newswriting, and fiction. Do not be misled by the momentum of dialogue, plot, or discussion. Pause in your reading to inquire, To what extent is this idea still true and cogent? Has there been a change in premises, events, circumstances? Am I in danger of being brainwashed into acceptance of new ideas because they have been joined with old ones? Why has the writer abandoned some considerations for others, or why has he continued to reiterate a theme or thesis from one stage of the work to another?

The political agitator and the representative of special interests in a society make effective use of the principle of momentum. A candidate or protégé, for example, may be portrayed at his best through a truthful but out-dated account of worthy deeds and self-sacrifice—and then, when the great issue at stake is about to be considered, the reader is inclined to follow in the footsteps of so kindly and self-sacrificing a person, who may be a genuine rascal. The propagandist becomes skilled in relating an abundance of minor facts or details, building the confidence of his readers, who become his victims as they unthinkingly accept his deceit. The reader must protect himself from the momentum of such a stream of ideas by testing them against experience, organizing them into commonsense categories of truths, half-truths, partial falsehoods, complete falsehoods, and questionable statements. The expert reader of literature, too, keeps a sharp eye on characters who behave "in character" and compares them with people in real life situations. Thus, he shows himself to be not only an experienced reader but also a true critic, for the two functions of reading and criticism accompany and complement each other.

In many works of fiction and drama, and in some poetry as well, the accumulation of unresolved dilemmas and complex events and information has the special effect of building psychological tension in the reader. Situations, characters, and unsolved problems multiply, taxing the memory, perhaps threatening to confuse the intellect and overburden the emotions. For this reason the skillful author interrupts the onward sweep of his plot by introducing light dialogue or humor or some diversionary episodes before carrying the central theme forward. If you can read an exciting mystery story or a play with enjoyment in a receptive, unruffled frame of mind despite repeated suspense and climaxes, you should thank the author whose creative artistry has made provision for the relief of mounting tension. Inferior works do not arouse intense feelings as do those masterpieces which require a breathing spell to interrupt the momentum of events. The author who creates a literary masterpiece sustains your interest by keeping you in suspense, absorbed in what is about to happen, just as a composer creates a melody that produces almost unbearable tension so long as it remains unfinished, the tension being relieved when the listener hears a satisfactory ending. Such an author understands and provides for the effects of momentum and the psychological reactions of his readers. His is the work you are likely to appreciate and enjoy.

Analogy. Most works of literature portray characters and situations which remind us of similar characters and situations we have encountered either in life or in our other reading. It has been said that there is nothing new under the sun and that the only new truths are the old ones. Nevertheless, there are also individuality and uniqueness in the creations of competent novelists, playwrights, and poets. As you read a literary work, analyze it to note any resemblance to other works, any similarities and differences between the characters and the people you have known or read about, and those qualities of theme or style which seem to you to be uniquely characteristic of the author.

Thus, in reading the Utopian works of Plato, Sir Thomas More, Francis Bacon, and Edward Bellamy, note the ways in which their ideal societies resemble and differ from one another: for example, the ideal community in Plato's *Republic* was a society of three rigid classes; in More's *Utopia* it meant a communistic life without any classes; in Bacon's vision it was a scientists' paradise; and in Bellamy's goal it was a socialistic commonwealth controlled by the state. Comparisons and contrasts of this kind sharpen critical analyses and deepen the understanding of literature.

Writers often utilize analogy in describing characters or in advocating ideas and points of view. Examine their analogies carefully to decide whether or not they are logically correct and reasonable and whether you should agree, disagree, or reserve judgment. Perhaps the comparison drawn between two people or between a person and some object in nature is actually distorted or unreasonable. Analogies to prove an argument may also be overdrawn or illogical. The writer may compare parental authority with autocratic rule, for instance, and he may ignore or minimize an important difference between the two while advocating that children should not be disciplined by their parents, the implication being that such display of authority would be as reprehensible as arbitrary dictatorship over a people. But an alert reader will notice crucial differences vitiating such analogies; for example, parental authority may be motivated by love of children instead of a desire to dominate over them. Critical readers should analyze analogies, detect special pleading based on faulty comparisons, and put the author's conclusions or implications to the severest test of logic and experience.

Emphasis. A skilled writer gives much more space to the important ideas and events in his work than he does to lesser ones, and the careful reader is expected to appreciate the reasons for these differences in emphasis. Of course, such a quantitative measurement is only a rough approximation and there are exceptions. A brief episode or even a significant brisk remark can sometimes change the entire trend of a plot or theme, especially if it comes at the climax to preceding sections. Nevertheless, unless he tries to evaluate variations in emphasis, the reader may underestimate the key points in a literary work or, for that matter, in any kind of written material. This principle is also applicable to news reports, essays, fiction, poetry, and drama.

In conversation, emphasis becomes apparent when the speaker raises his voice, repeats an idea, or makes use of gestures. (The humorous reference to a gossip who could be kept quiet only by tying her hands has an element of truth in it.) In reading, the author may include these same indications of emphasis indirectly by describing or referring to them, but more commonly the absence of direct clues as to the relative importance of any part compels the reader to search for and evaluate the significant elements. Reading the views of book reviewers and critics or discussion with other readers can often help to illuminate the relative importance of different ideas, characters, and events in a work of literature, but the reader should arrive at his own independent judgment based upon his analysis of the work itself. In some instances, he may feel that the author has overemphasized by excessive, tiresome repetition or superfluous discussion. You should appreciate the author's intent and read his work sympathetically, yet after so doing, feel free to criticize and consider whether a change in emphasis might not have made the work more interesting and true to life. Always the question to ask is: Why did this or that character, episode, idea, or argument receive so much or so little attention and emphasis?

Implication. The experienced author knows how to suggest ideas forcefully to readers without stating them directly. What he writes may carry a significant implication with it, a hint of additional meanings or of possible future events. The reader is expected to read between the lines, accepting impressions and views based upon subtle cues instead of specific information and evidence. Implication can take on a dramatic, evasive form, as in the biblical story of Cain and Abel, in which Cain, having slain Abel his brother, replied to God's query about the whereabouts of Abel, "I know not; am I my brother's keeper?" implying he did not know *because* it was not his duty to watch over his brother. The reply implies much more about Cain's character than a simple direct statement, "I know not," would have revealed. Very often the subtleties in great poetry imply also a wide range of possible interpretations, some of them intricate and almost inexpressible in words. The sensitive poet's choice of words, rhythm, imagery, alliteration, and sequence of ideas, and his use of repetition, contrast, and allusion all contribute to the total effect of his implied moods and meanings.

By striving to explore the implications of an author's words, the reader adds the power of his own imagination and in effect participates in bringing the work to a satisfying conclusion or state of effectiveness. An example of a simple conclusion implied by the ideas of a fictional character is the following paragraph from *Huckleberry Finn*, which implies that prayer is only a gesture in futility—a point of view which Mark Twain himself shared:

> I says to myself, if a body can get anything they pray for, why don't Deacon Winn get back the money he lost on pork? Why can't the widow get back her silver snuffbox that was stole? Why can't Miss Watson fat up? No, says I to myself, there ain't nothing in it. I went and told the widow about it, and she said the thing a body could

get by praying for it was "spiritual gifts." This was too many for me, but she told me what she meant—I must help other people, and look out for them all the time, and never think about myself. This was including Miss Watson, as I took it. I went out in the woods and turned it over in my mind a long time, but I couldn't see no advantage about it—except for other people; so at last I reckoned I wouldn't worry about it any more, but just let it go.

Mark Twain stated the same conclusion explicitly in his own notebook, as follows:

I do not believe in special providences. I believe that the universe is governed by strict and immutable laws. If one man's family is swept away by a pestilence and another man's is spared it is only the law working: God is not interfering in that small matter, either against the one man or in favor of the other. . . . If I break . . . moral laws I cannot see how I injure God by it, for He is beyond the reach of injury by me—I could as easily injure a planet by throwing mud at it. (A. B. Paine, *Mark Twain: A Biography*)

The words of Huck Finn which imply the author's disbelief in prayer are more persuasive than Twain's own statement. What an author implies in the words of his characters can be more convincing than what he directly states.

ANALYSIS OF PROPAGANDA

Propaganda is the use of language to influence the minds of men. Its most gullible victims are those readers who have developed excessive confidence in the printed word. The expert reader recognizes propaganda in many kinds of reading materials and knows how to deal with it. He reads critically in self-defense and depends upon his own earnest analysis and judgment before accepting ideas or conclusions.

Propagandists may be well-intentioned. But even gifted, sincere writers can misinterpret our world, sometimes more than those of us who read their eloquent words with admiration. I recall writing to the eminent playwright

George Bernard Shaw for his interpretation of Nazi totalitarianism and for suggestions to prevent its spread, and he replied (June 2, 1934) that he sympathized with Mr. Hitler "on nearly every point except the quaint notions of ethnology and biology which he seems to have picked up at an impressionable age from Houston Chamberlain's fascinating and suggestive but fundamentally imaginative and unhistorical work called The Foundations of the Nineteenth Century." True, Hitler was undoubtedly misled by his reading of the Chamberlain propaganda, but if a keen student of the human condition like Shaw could also be so tragically deceived by Hitler's own propaganda into misinterpreting political and social realities, obviously we, being less experienced interpreters, must take special care not to be similarly misled into making grave errors of judgment. It is far better to doubt all works and ideas than it would be to accept them blindly, better to analyze than to swallow uncritically, better to dissect than to embrace without prudent investigation and critical evaluation.

During the 1930s and 1940s, pioneering studies in the analysis of propaganda were contributed by Professor Clyde R. Miller of Columbia University, who had inaugurated courses in this field at the university and had later served as a founder and secretary of the Institute for Propaganda Analysis. Dr. Miller summarized seven basic propaganda devices in his *The Process of Persuasion* as card-stacking, name-calling, glittering generality, transfer, testimonial, plain folks, and bandwagon—devices which have been widely accepted as the most common techniques of the propagandist.

Dr. Miller's list of devices may be explained as follows: *cardstacking*, arranging plausible assertions in a sequence to trap the reader into accepting them and rejecting contrary statements; *name-calling*, attaching a contemptuous label to a proposition, thereby inducing the reader to reject it; *glittering generality*, making a flat assertion or broad assumption repeated as often as necessary to impel acceptance without critical analysis; *transfer*, associating the reputation of a respected person, tradition, or institution with propaganda so that readers will be inclined to accept it; *testimonial,* citing the approval of authorities to induce acceptance of propaganda; *plain folks,* making an appeal based on the desire of readers to follow the traditional practices and ideas of their group and thus avoid eccentric or exceptional behavior; *bandwagon,* making an appeal to join the winning team or crowd in their acceptance of propaganda.

There are several ways to analyze propaganda. We may consider the subject from the points of view of the sociologist, the psychologist, and the linguist, respectively. The sociologist investigates the use of propaganda as a means of controlling social institutions and public opinion and policy. The psychologist seeks to track down the effects of propaganda upon the thinking and behavior of individuals. The linguist studies the language of propaganda as a method of persuasion. Readers will be better prepared to cope with propagandist writings if they become familiar with all three points of view towards propaganda.

The Sociology of Propaganda. Language is essential to human association and survival. The members of any society must exchange information and share ideas by oral or written communication. Such exchange and sharing are part of the normal process of satisfying elementary human wants. Propaganda surpasses commonplace types of communication and applies forceful, convincing language to influence people and control their reactions. To accomplish these purposes, the propagandist attracts the serious attention of his audience, sustains their favorable interest in his message, which he must make as clear, simple, and emphatic as possible, and presents assertions and evidence which will appeal to the recipients and be accepted by them as means of attaining their own goals.

Sources of Propaganda. In assessing the impact of propaganda upon ourselves, we need to know the sources from which such materials emanate. We are in danger of becoming innocent victims unless we investigate these sources and their output. The first question to ask, then, is, from the sociologist's point of view: Who are the propagandists?

Propaganda is constantly being poured into newspapers, periodicals, pamphlets, and books by all sorts of groups, including business associations, unions, political parties, government agencies, civic associations, international organizations, and the professions. Fortunately, publishers have been on the alert to prevent censorship and to maintain a free press as a marketplace of competing information and ideas. The reporting of every conceivable type of news and opinion makes it possible for readers to evaluate all points of view in printed materials without restriction—if they take the time and trouble to do so. On the other hand, publishers must attract their audiences and at the same time retain the goodwill of merchants and advertisers. As a consumer of the printed word, therefore, it is up to the reader to strike a balance between no-truths, half-truths, and whole truths, without swallowing extremist doctrines which may have a superficial appeal because of their dogmatic simplicity. Readers of newspapers cannot expect them to disclose that a particular advertisement is concealing facts or that a news handout by the government is self-serving, incomplete, or inaccurate. They need the built-in protection of their own reading attitudes and skills. They need to understand, evaluate, and counteract the principal techniques of the propagandist, yet they must be just and fair to his point of view.

Consider, for example, the propaganda for and against the legal and medical professions, whose honorable traditions and service to mankind go back to antiquity. Today, attorneys and physicians are sensitive to criticism, for they prefer to handle mischievous procedures quietly, "within the club." Consequently, the public has too often formed a low opinion of these professions, generally unaware that the medical societies and bar associations have been working very diligently to eradicate shortcom-

ings and bring everyday practices into conformity with
the highest ethical standards. The public does not hear
about these constructive efforts, but only about cases in
which a successful plaintiff obtained little compensation
for his serious injury or losses and expenses while his
lawyer received an excellent return without substantial
service of any kind. The public knows little about the
heavy overhead costs of attorneys, the wasted time because of court congestion, delays by ingenious opposing
counsel, and the lack of dependable employees, and
sees only that the system of law and justice has become
inefficient, expensive, and sometimes even corrupt, that
the wealthy man willing to pay an experienced, clever
attorney has an advantage over the less affluent citizen.
Justice is at best dubious under these circumstances.

It may be true that the majority of persons defeated
or convicted in court proceedings deserve their fate, but
this defense of inefficiency does not satisfy the critical
reader, who knows that persons with limited means
cannot employ numerous investigators and attorneys
to represent them, that such persons, in civil cases, compete with powerful adversaries, that innocent persons,
in criminal cases, are often convicted owing to insuffi-
cient funds for investigators and skilled counsel or actual
neglect and negligence by disinterested counsel, that if
convicted such persons frequently are unable to appeal
or to prove extenuating circumstances and good character, and therefore often receive severe penalties (imprisonment for minor offenses is not unknown) while
wealthy defendants delay or even defy justice with im-
punity. Leaders in the profession are among the first
to point out that the judicial system should not be turned
into a one-sided affair in which justice (ideally depicted
as blind to artificial conditions) depends upon the individual's power, influence, class, or race—wealth or
status—in society.

The propaganda of physicians, who are also reluctant
to publicize the evils afflicting their profession, is likely
to be as one-sided as the propaganda directed against

their profession. Medical education has been costly, and physicians resent interference by the public which might endanger their opportunity to recoup substantial investments in medical education and might impede their efforts to serve their patients expertly while enjoying that high standard of material comfort which they deserve. Concerning an admitted shortage of skilled physicians, they point out correctly that reduced fees and lower earnings would merely discourage talented young people from entering the profession. Well-trained doctors possess considerable technical knowledge and useful means of diagnosis and therapy, and many of them attempt to practice the ethical standards of their calling, to put service to patients ahead of their own gain and convenience. Nevertheless, the medical professions are plagued with conditions of scarcity of qualified personnel, excessive costs and fees, overwork, and poor rapport with patients, who, in turn, tend to regard the physician as a businessman waiting to be paid handsomely by insured clients or by government agencies. Even those increasing numbers of dedicated doctors who employ adequate skills and medicines carefully and effectively are extremely busy and often fail to inform patients about the details of the medicines being prescribed under brand names or the accomplishments and problems of the profession. Some physicians depend on a mysterious air of busy authority to impress their patients, who eventually grow suspicious and resentful. Millions of people resort to self-treatment or to quackery. Other millions are simply careless, irresponsible victims, including six million alcoholics and multitudes of drug addicts, ignoring or rejecting medical advice, apparently willing to risk chronic illness from obesity, smoking, drinking, or other self-abuses. The reader should consider these sad realities when reading propaganda against physicians as well as the defensive propaganda of the profession.

MOTIVES FOR PROPAGANDA. Readers need to consider not only who are the propagandists but also what are their motives for the dissemination of propaganda. In the case of business organizations the motive is one of profit-making, and that can be a quite worthy one if based on honorable standards of conduct. It is most regrettable and dangerous, however, when propaganda is devised to protect the power and increase the profits of unethical enterprises.

Thus, the American public has long been disturbed by the high incidence of automobile accident fatalities— a total of 56,000 annually. Many causes have been cited for this appalling situation, such as drunken driving, improperly constructed roads, incompetent or careless or discourteous drivers, and defective automobiles or tires. When the writer Ralph Nader investigated the situation and attributed many of the accidents to unsafe vehicles, a leading automobile manufacturer attempted to silence him. Detectives were employed to observe Mr. Nader and report any behavior which might be used to discredit his reputation or compel him to cease his criticisms of the industry. When this effort at censorship was exposed, the American reader became fully aware of Mr. Nader's sincerity and the real motives behind the manufacturer's activities—the willingness to go to any lengths to protect profits even at the cost of thousands of lives sacrificed because of defective vehicles. Eventually the federal government required automobile manufacturers to make public periodic reports concerning hundreds of thousands of defective cars recalled for repair. Alert readers will henceforth have no confidence in the pronouncements of automobile manufacturers, and this consequence will be most unfortunate, for certainly the industry as a whole does not wish to deceive its millions of customers. Like most other business enterprises, that industry can remain prosperous and still tell the truth, the whole truth, while earning handsome profits for shareholders, paying satisfactory wages to employees, and saving thousands of lives annually by admitting deficiencies and taking appropriate remedial action, such as manufacturing much sturdier, safer vehicles, going far beyond the very few standards set by slow-moving government agencies.

Readers can, if they will, detect the motives and nullify the efforts of propagandists. Thus they know that the leaders of political parties aim to control appointments and to obtain lucrative contracts or other favors from elected candidates; that the managers of large corporations and their advertising agencies are interested in increasing sales and profits; that labor organizations attempt to win public support for higher wages and to increase their membership; that universities issue rosy reports about their services and plans in order to extract funds from alumni; that the directors of health associations publish half-truths about accomplishments or potentialities in the hope that additional money, prestige, and public support will enable them to expand their enterprises. Readers cannot expect such propagandists to disclose their wasteful practices, shortcomings, or mistakes. Many worthy causes suffer because skeptical readers have become resistant to all propaganda. More and more readers are becoming immune to the tons of propaganda, good, partly good, or evil, to which they are constantly being subjected. Increasingly, they demand, and should demand, an answer to the question, *What have you, the propagandist, really accomplished for the betterment of conditions?*

The Psychology of Propaganda. Masterpieces of literature influence the reader through appeals to his emotions as well as to his reason. They awaken in him sympathy, admiration, or pity for the characters being portrayed, and often feelings of wonder, pleasure, or gratification from reading about places and events in such works. But there is no attempt to mislead the reader with half-truths, concealment of facts, or deliberate falsehoods. On the contrary, the creative writer exposes his fictitious characters to the light of day and invites the reader to explore the truth, the whole truth, about people, places, and events. Quite different are the motives and techniques of the propagandist, who deliberately attempts to arouse in the reader emotions of fear or excessive pride, feelings of inferiority or superiority, anger, envy, hatred, uncertainty, and frustration, thus easily beguiling him to accept fallacies or irrational views.

THE APPEAL TO AUTHORITY. A reader burdened with a feeling of inferiority is likely, for example, to be susceptible to propaganda based on authority. Approval by an authority makes him more confident about his own ideas. When I was a young student, I was often guilty of accepting some idea merely because an "eminent" person had approved it. But one eminent philosopher, Ralph Barton Perry, of Harvard University, cured me of that habit by asking for my authority and then asking who would be the authority for that authority. He pointed out that such an appeal would carry us back to an endless list of authorities and would leave no time for examination of the idea itself. It is true, of course, that ideas developed by people highly experienced in a relevant field of knowledge are worthy of the reader's attention, but never are they worthy of acceptance without criticism, investigation, and independent judgment. On most subjects there are conflicting authorities, none of whom is always right about everything. The expert in one field is often sadly mistaken in another. Beware, too, of the propagandist who cites common knowledge in support of his idea, beginning with "As everyone knows, such and such is the case." He is appealing to your natural desire to behave like all other intelligent people by accepting his statements, which may actually consist of half-truths or false assertions rejected by most people.

Authorities such as physicians and other professionals seem to be particularly susceptible to the propaganda of their own authorities. An amusing consequence of the blind acceptance of medical authority is related in Molière's comedy, *Love Is a Doctor,* in which it is reported that a sick coachman has suddenly died. But the physician in attendance refused to believe that his patient had died and had been buried, for the patient had been ill for only six days and, according to the great authority Hippocrates, such an illness could not end during the first thirteen days. "Well, well," was the commonsense reply, "Hippocrates or no Hippocrates, the coachman is dead."

FLATTERY. Flattery is another common technique of the clever propagandist. This appeal is effective among readers with a feeling of superiority. They like to be flattered because flattery reinforces their claim to superior intelligence. Hitler's propaganda was based on this appeal addressed to the German people, who felt that they were superior human beings constituting a "master race." In such propaganda the readers are reminded of their "special" virtues, power, and knowledge and praised for their ability to understand and appreciate the propagandist's ideas. The propagandist implies that only a select group will really be able to comprehend the full significance of his views, but that you, the superior reader, will of course understand everything without difficulty, even though you are only one among many thousands of his readers, all of whom are being reminded that they are superior to others and particularly to all "outsiders," or foreigners, or opponents. Flattery works too often because you the reader may at the time be perhaps weary of problems, susceptible to being patted on the shoulder by someone whose words will pacify you, provide some carefree illusion, and strengthen your self-assurance. The alert reader should detect flattery promptly and resist such an ingenious attempt to stifle his power of independent judgment.

GULLIBILITY. There are many other psychological appeals used by propagandists. For example, the newspaper columnist may try to form an intellectual partnership with readers, taking them into his confidence by revealing "secret" information shared only with millions of other readers; the politician may appeal to the readers' feelings of generosity and sympathy, confessing that his proposal is not perfect but the best he has been able to do so far; the advertising genius may inform readers that for years some lady endured illness and pain until suddenly a neighbor introduced her to the remarkable headache powder being advertised—so, you readers, too, can be cured with the same patent medicine. The propagandist who wants to shake the confidence of the reader in some idea may humbly confess that he used to think that way, too, but changed his mind as a result of hard experience. Contradictory arguments may be presented to confuse the reader until he is ready to accept a one-sided, plausible conclusion. The reader's best protection against all these psychological appeals of the propagandist is the intellectual armor of complete skepticism, perhaps best expressed in the challenging retort, *I'm from Missouri; show me!*

Of course, writers often make legitimate, constructive use of psychological appeals. Thus, I have myself frankly confessed youthful adherence to erroneous notions since abandoned, and there is no harm in so informing sympathetic readers and encouraging emulation. At one time I was even gullible enough to accept the absurd claim of a prominent advertising-oriented psychologist that his then unique attempts to associate a product being advertised with the subconscious longings and psychological susceptibilities of consumers were morally justifiable. I was gullible enough to edit and publish his book explaining the techniques he used. In later years I realized that it is ethically wrong to advertise a soap by appealing to the reader's nobility of soul, his faith in chastity and purity as exemplified by the whiteness of the soap, for I knew that the competing soaps were quite as good though not so pure in color. Confessing my mistake, I trusted that confession is good for the soul and good for the dissemination of the truth.

PROPAGANDA FOR PROPAGANDA. One defense offered for the use of ingenious, misleading psychological appeals in propaganda and advertising is the assertion that the public is getting only what it wants or is willing to accept. The question arises, If readers display poor taste in books, for instance, is that because trashy materials have popularized low standards, or are the trashy materials being made available because many readers have already developed low standards otherwise and now demand them? Both views are probably partly true. But I am reminded of those automobile manufacturers who produce costly oversized unsafe cars which they advertise through psychological appeals to the consumer based on his feeling of superiority over his neighbors, thus reinforcing his reprehensible attitude (often a form of compensation for repressed feelings of insecurity and inferiority). Then the same manufacturers have the effrontery to claim that they are merely giving the consumer what he wants and demands from them! If the reader of offensive advertisements of this kind can be made to realize what the advertisers are trying to do— beguile him by taking advantage of his psychological weaknesses—and if he can become sufficiently skeptical and fact-minded, a critical reader, he will perhaps turn away from the advertisements and also reject the misrepresented products advertised. He will then get what he really wants and needs, namely, honest, full information in advertisements and genuinely superior products at reasonable prices.

Not all advertising is deceptive; nevertheless, the reader should always be skeptical enough to detect abuses. In this respect the book industry has an exceptionally good record. Publishers have generally observed high standards in the publication and promotion of literature. In response to the expectations and discriminating tastes of experienced readers, they continually strive to improve their product as well as their advertising appeals. There are many conscientious writers and ethical advertisers and distributors of books. A great deal of the writing in newspapers, journals, and books is well-intentioned, constructive, and well-balanced, even when it includes emphatic appeals to the reader's pride and sympathies. As for the hucksters, in the last analysis if enough readers become aware of what the propagandists are attempting to accomplish and analyze their appeals severely, there will soon be an end to the flood of one-sided, deceptive, "mismotivated" forms of propaganda and advertising.

The Language of Propaganda. The propagandist influences readers by means of language skills applied in accordance with a definite strategy. He takes into account the sad immoral conditions of the time, knowing that many people have become so accustomed to deceiving others and to being deceived by others that a truly honest appeal would come as a shock, something almost unbelievable. He can always count on enough psychologically weak or gullible victims to bring him considerable success.

Familiar Devices. Among the age-old language devices still in wide use are those of repetition of statements without evidence; exaggeration; understatement of opposing views; diversion of critical thought through humor or sarcasm; and omission of facts. When the skilled propagandist repeats an idea, he varies the words to avoid monotony and to convince more readers, for he knows that some words will appeal to one reader while others will convince another. Exaggeration and understatement are not overdone, but are applied gradually and subtly; so, too, are humor and sarcasm, which might otherwise distract the reader's attention from the propaganda message. Omission of unfavorable information must often be accompanied by extensive discussion of the propagandist's own proposition in order to obscure or conceal the omissions.

Other Linguistic Tricks. Misquoting is another old device, especially effective when statements are taken out of context to change the original meaning of the quote. Ambiguous or vague statements often help to deceive readers—for example, statements about merchandise being "guaranteed or your money back," when there is no elucidation of what the guarantee covers. Dubious, unproved assertions are used as the basis for unjustifiable conclusions, as, for instance, in the statements: "The tax rate in our town is unfair. If the new schools are built, the unbearable taxes will never be reduced." (Note that *unfair* in the first sentence becomes *unbearable* in the second.) In such ambiguities, two of the most common misused words are *because* and *average*. The fact that night follows day does not mean that night causes day, but the propagandist often mixes up cause and mere sequence. An average is misleading unless fully explained: thus, if one man earns $10 while another earns $50, the average is $30, but the statement that the average earnings are $30 is misleading, since neither man earns anything like that amount. Readers need to be always alert to counteract these linguistic tricks of the propagandist.

The Miseducation of Propagandists. The propagandist's deceitful habits are learned chiefly in the home and community. Schools and colleges do what they can to raise standards of language usage, but in general they have been more successful in teaching future propagandists to master the linguistic tools of their trade than they have been in teaching them the ethical use of such tools.

Of course, the strategy of modern propagandists and hucksters is nothing new. It is the same as the very ancient strategy of all scoundrels throughout history, as expressed and advocated by Machiavelli in *The Prince* (1532) when he advised rulers to be cunning like a fox, never honest or compassionate, or faithful, humane, or sincere, but always to seem so, for that is the way to convince people that their leader is a good person who means them well. To become a successful leader, you must be a hypocrite and dissembler, said Machiavelli, for that is the only way to control the minds of the people, who are simple-minded souls unable to see beyond their noses. He assumed, moreover, that the common people are themselves greedy and corrupt and that they would betray their leaders and one another, too, if they could get away with it. He said that the ruler should therefore never hesitate to mislead them into believing him to be a saint, for very few would be clever enough to discover his true character, and the masses would richly deserve their fate. Today the propagandist is merely implementing Machiavelli's advice in a sophisticated way, taking advantage of troubled minds and misusing the ideas of psychologists such as Pavlov, Adler, and Freud. Indeed, the deceitful strategy of the propagandist has become universal throughout the occupations and human relationships of our society. It is the primary cause of man's persistent problems of war, poverty, and crime, and the true cause of the revolt of idealistic youth against the institutions, standards, and customs of the older generation.

5

How To Discover
The Truth

Reading is a primary road to learning, to the discovery of the truth. The spoken word is useful, but it is fleeting, quickly heard and gone, replaced by other words. But printed words remain at the reader's disposal, waiting to be understood, and are subject to repeated examination and interpretation. Many spoken words are impromptu, often thoughtless or unfounded, whereas printed words reflect the author's experience and technical skill. Therefore careful reading of newspapers, journals, and books can mold the minds and enrich the personalities of old and new generations alike.

The cause of reading has its foes and friends, its roadblocks and gateways to learning the truth. Among the roadblocks are censorship, misinformation, and habits of uncritical reading. Among the friends who hold open the gateways to learning are the libraries and bookstores, the governmental, social, and scientific organizations, and the schools and universities. These friends of reading are the promoters of light and knowledge pitted against the forces of darkness and ignorance.

CENSORSHIP

Censorship represents the authoritarian view that certain individuals should decide what is best for other people to read and, therefore, to think and believe.

89

Censorship is based on the notion that self-appointed or selected authorities should prescribe limits on the freedom to write and to read, deciding what is good and pure and wholesome for all. They are to be the maîtres d'hôtel who present us with an intellectual menu from which we as humble diners are to make a choice under their watchful supervision.

What would happen if censors could eventually discover what is truly good and pure and what is evil and impure in the realm of ideas and could then compel us to accept their decisions? If all our books thereafter contained only good and pure ideas and information, would corruption, greed, and falsehood be eliminated? If not, then our purified books would deprive us of any means of learning about such evils as they exist in our world and thus any hope of evaluating and rejecting loathsome ideas and practices. Since these purified books would give us a distorted view of the world, quite contrary to life as it exists in our society, they would only teach us untruths, misleading us, and there would be no value in reading them.

From the earliest years of childhood, the minds of men are molded by models in their homes and communities. The feignedly pious, self-deceiving parent who would suppress the thoughts of children, as of adults, is the very person who sets an example of autocracy, unreasonableness, deceit, and hypocrisy. It is he who needs to be re-educated so that he will think critically as he reads and will teach his children to develop critical judgment and self-direction. Guidance and good example are essential, but any form of censorship is a confession of the failure of society to produce a generation of honest, critical readers qualified to discriminate between wholesome and corrupt literature.

Some well-intentioned people, believing that "evil" writings may increase a reader's tendency to commit immoral or criminal acts advocate censorship by government agencies. These well-meaning persons mistakenly assume that prohibition will improve character or prevent the deterioration of character. On the contrary, repression destroys every possibility of character development. Guidance toward discovery, and acceptance, of the truth builds character. Books must not be distortions; they must reveal all the good and evil in society if readers are to learn anything from them and if there is to be any hope of social improvement.

If large numbers of the population prefer slipshod, salacious, or dishonest newspapers, journals, films, and books, this is a danger signal indeed, a warning not that repressive laws must be passed but that the real causes of deceit and depravity must be revealed and counteracted, causes such as commercial greed, excessive competition for profits, injustice, parental and educational neglect, poverty, and, above all, hypocrisy—that observable contrast between national ideals and collective behavior, the same hypocrisy that argues for the censorship of books. Let the censors therefore seal their own lips and censor themselves instead of attempting to control the minds of their equals or betters in our society—the creative minds of writers and the critical minds of alert readers.

If there is censorship anywhere, there can be no faith in literature, no opportunity for the reader to evaluate literature and decide for himself the genuine worth of printed materials. Under censorship there can be no critical, intelligent reading and therefore no honest, intelligent citizenship. The existence of censorship in any community is a barometer of its lack of culture, a shameful proclamation that its adult citizens cannot be trusted to discriminate intelligently, to think straight, to display good taste, to live decently, and to grow in the power of critical reading.

In the books of the Holy Bible, the ancient prophets of Israel presented the facts of evil together with the good, including obscenity, venality, treachery, violence, treason, human sacrifice, idolatry, murder, adultery, and almost every conceivable crime. These were to be taken to heart by youth and adults alike. The founders of the United States of America realized that all men must have freedom to seek the truth and to know and reject evil, and that meant absolute freedom to write and to read anything in the realm of ideas. They inserted a guarantee in the Constitution, forbidding any law "abridging the freedom of speech, or of the press," for they had studied history and had also had experience with oppressive authorities threatening to control their minds and institutions. The language of the United States Constitution is simple, unqualified, precise, unmistakable in meaning and intent. It does not say, as can be pointed out to fearful lawmakers and jurists, that freedom of the press can be abridged if the writing is accompanied by salacious advertising or base appeals to depraved tastes. It says in plain language anyone can understand that there shall be no abridgment whatever, that is to say, no political control over the communication of ideas, so that even speech or writing widely considered harmful to the state must be tolerated. To forbid a single word of an individual means to abridge the freedom of speech or press of all citizens. The Constitution does not forbid some reasonable regulation of the time or place for public speeches, but it does forbid all regulations which prevent anyone from expressing his ideas to anyone else willing to listen or read. (Legally, freedom of the press carries with it the freedom to read, for there would be no writing at all without readers. Communication of ideas is meaningless unless the audience has freedom to hear or to read them.)

The proper alternative to repressive censorship is to encourage by purchase and merited acclaim the publication of more and more good books which people will insist on reading and evaluating for themselves. The heavy hand of censorship smothers the minds of men, deprives them of the intellectual air which they must have for mental development, and stifles their independent thinking. Even the young need abundant opportunity to detect evil and replace it with wholesome experience, to develop taste and appreciation by critically evaluating, within the limits of their growing capacity, and for valid reasons rejecting falsehood, partial truths, depravity, greed, and bigotry. Only those men who read and analyze ideas without restrictions can be trusted to despise evil and to develop high standards of judgment and morality. When men have too often been deprived of the right and opportunity to evaluate ideas, they behave stupidly or irrationally and accept like sheep such despicable evils as censors and censorship. Freedom to write and to read as we please is the cornerstone of our democratic way of life.

Certain legal experts have sometimes defended a limited censorship of speech and press by asserting irrelevant arguments, such as, "No one has the right to shout 'Fire!' in a crowded theater," or "No one has a right to print a libel or endanger the safety of the nation." All such arguments are deliberate evasions of the issue and bear no pertinence whatever to our constitutional guarantees of free speech and a free press, which protect the right of all the people to hear and read any ideas about their institutions and mode of society, without limitation, and to judge for themselves which ideas are worth considering or accepting as the basis for public policy, taste, and preference. Freedom of speech and freedom of the press have nothing to do with using a printed page to set fire (directly or indirectly) to a theater, with defaming the character or invading the privacy of a citizen. They are basic rights which must not be restricted, and those who would in any degree abridge them—whether lowly demagogues or high jurists—show little faith in the judgments of the people and truly endanger the cause of freedom and the nation itself.

MISINFORMATION

Incorrect information is often partly true. Propagandists, for example, spice false assertions with a little truth, sweeten the bitter with a bit of honey. But misinformation can be spread innocently, carelessly, by other writers as well. Certain types of evasion and deception have become fashionable and so common that readers need to be always on guard to counteract them, even in such ordinary material as weather reports. Direct predictions of rain or sunshine, of warm and sunny weather, or of cold and wet weather, are a thing of the past. Today the weather reports indicate that there is a 10 percent chance of rain, or that it will be partly cloudy, or partly sunny. Such predictions can scarcely be wrong. If it rains, the 10 percent chance of rain has happened; if it does not rain, the 90 percent chance of fair weather has come to pass. The weather reporter should give us the old-type honest prediction, "It will rain tomorrow," and if it does not rain, frankly admit his error.

Not only weather reports and routine news announcements but more important official government statements can be quite misleading. I recall preparing a research study about the educational system of a foreign country, depending heavily upon information supplied by its government. Later I discovered that the data could not possibly be correct, for no combination of the statistics added up to the required totals. I wrote to the foreign consulate about the discrepancies as well as various contradictions between the alleged facts and broad conclusions in the government literature, and was eventually informed that all the errors and deficiencies were due entirely to clerical mistakes! In most countries, there is a lack of information about innumerable matters and guesswork is unavoidable, but it should be labelled as estimates, not as verifiable truths.

It is unfortunate that most readers do not have an opportunity to consult original sources. Information is apt to be secondhand, borrowed by careless writers from reliable scientific and professional journals, but taken out of context and distorted in newspapers or magazines, much to the dismay of the original investigators. Scientific publications report thousands of preliminary researches or experiments in the fields of health and medicine, psychology, and physical sciences. Then reporters and feature writers eager to attract more readers select those reports which can be converted into spectacular news. It is no wonder that readers are becoming disillusioned about all such information, for they read about highly-promising, sensational new developments and discoveries, yet never hear about them again. Critical-minded readers no longer believe such reports, not even those with little exaggeration, for they have been too often misled. Readers have grown more and more skeptical; before accepting stories about significant contributions to human well-being, they demand evidence, particularly the scientist's own statements about his work, which always contain cautious qualifications and reservations. Alert readers analyze all news accounts carefully and in most instances are compelled to conclude that there is little of value in sensational reports.

UNCRITICAL READING

It may seem odd to assert that a great deal of misinformation is manufactured by the reader himself while he is reading. Ask several people to read a news report about some controversial subject, and after reading it they will give you a variety of interpretations. Each will omit what is of little interest to him, emphasize what he likes, and slight or perhaps ignore the important points he dislikes or disbelieves. To read critically, you must look within yourself, become aware of your own bias or assumptions, and interpret the material, not as a means of reinforcing your past prejudices and conclusions, but as a method of discovering what the writer really intended you to learn from his words.

Uncritical reading results in misconceptions, misinterpretations, of the author's ideas. Not only is the ordinary reader too often guilty of hasty conclusions because he fails to study the author's work, but even the best-known literary critics and book reviewers have sometimes been rightly accused of failure to read thoroughly and carefully. Not all reviewers have the necessary time and patience to give books the comprehensive analysis they deserve; some betray their trust, reading only a few pages to obtain a partial or incorrect view of a book, and on this basis recommend or disparage it. The best reviewers, however, insist upon reading and rereading a book before evaluating it. They feel an obligation to guide their audience wisely and strive to provide a well-balanced appraisal. Every reader should follow the example of such reviewers by asking himself what is new, old, unusual, good, bad, most provocative and interesting in their reading material. Fortunate is the reader who finds sufficient reason in his reading to modify his own ideas, for that is evidence of value received, the most that any author can do for his readers.

LIBRARIES AND BOOKSTORES

The most useful things in the world are free, such as loyal friends, peace of mind, agreeable conversation, appreciation of music and art, and the opportunity to read fine books in public libraries. Next to the books you own and treasure, those in the public library can be the greatest source of pleasure and fulfillment. The library is the foremost gateway to freedom and truth. Do you make full use of your library?

Library Resources. Currently the number of libraries in the United States exceeds 28,000, of which nearly 12,000 are free public libraries of local communities. There are thousands of school, college, and university libraries, as well as more than 5,000 special libraries, including medical, technical, industrial, business, and miscellaneous private libraries. The largest library is the Library of Congress, with its 13½ million books and pamphlets; next to the largest is the New York Public Library, with its 7½ million books. These two libraries alone possess more books than most nations have at their disposal. Very few countries have free public library systems comparable to those in the United States on the basis of population, although substantial library facilities are readily accessible to readers at little or no cost in the British and Scandinavian countries. The Soviet Union is reported to have as many as 400,000 libraries, among which are the Lenin State Library with 15 million books and pamphlets, the Leningrad Public Library with 10 million books, and the library of the Academy of Sciences with 8 million volumes. The Soviet libraries are, of course, state institutions which must provide many millions of copies of books for the dissemination of state political doctrines; nevertheless, the current reported total of nearly 2 billion volumes represents a remarkable achievement.

Readers who use typical American public libraries are provided with stimulating ideas and information, quiet relaxation, and communion with gifted authors, past and present, representing all conceivable points of view. Library materials include all sorts of periodicals and pamphlets, historical documents, government publications, and educational, recreational, and reference books. The library usually has comfortable accommodations for reading, convenient procedures to borrow books, and competent guidance and advice for readers. Books are classified into groups corresponding to ten subject areas covering all fields of knowledge so that any reader can easily find information in philosophy, psychology, religion, all the social sciences, philology, science, the useful arts, the fine arts, literature, and history, as well as miscellaneous sources, such as encyclopedias. Many libraries participate in a regional system, so that books not available in one library can easily be obtained for the reader from some other library in the system. Most readers can find the materials they need either in or through their nearby library, but if they cannot do so on occasion, they can always inquire where the desired information may be obtained. Thus, if you wish reports of researches in a special field, such as health or medicine, the librarian can usually give you the names and addresses of specialized journals or associations to which you can write for such reports.

Periodical indexes in the library—for example, the *Reader's Guide to Periodical Literature* (for 100 American and Canadian journals) and the *International Index* (for over 250 American and foreign scholarly journals)—index articles in magazines. There are various subject indexes, such as the *Education Index* (for teachers). There are indexes to all the news reported in the *New York Times*. Valuable information about books can be found in the *Book Review Digest*, which reprints excerpts from reviewers' comments about current books. Encyclopedias, such as the *Britannica, Americana, Colliers, Columbia, Grolier Universal*, and *World Book*, are filled with useful information, as are certain widely used reference books, namely, *Statistical Abstracts* (for data about United States institutions, business, etc.), the *Statesmen's Yearbook* (for data about foreign countries), the *World Almanac*, the *New York Times Encyclopedic Almanac*, and the *Information Please Almanac*, and numerous gazetteers, atlases, dictionaries, travel guidebooks, and reference books about reference books (such as the excellent volume, *Basic Reference Books*, by Louis Shores). *Webster's Geographical Dictionary, Webster's Biographical Dictionary*, Edward C. Smith and Arnold J. Zurcher's *Dictionary of American Politics*, and Harold S. Sloan and Arnold J. Zurcher's *Dictionary of Economics* are particularly useful sources of accurate data. There can be no reason for American readers to complain about the accessibility of information and ideas in the public libraries.

Librarians have been in the forefront in the continuous battle for the right of citizens to read whatever they please. Bookstores, too, defend this basic American principle, but sometimes booksellers are plagued with narrowminded, prejudiced individuals who have so little faith in the American way of freedom that they object to the sale of books with which they disagree. Occasionally booksellers may withdraw such books because they must earn a profit to remain in business and they fear the loss of trade— though most booksellers refuse to yield to this form of intellectual blackmail. Rare indeed is the librarian who will bow to such un-American pressures. The librarians welcome books expressing many different points of view and will generally be pleased to order controversial books requested by readers if sufficient funds are made available for this purpose.

Libraries, together with bookstores and schools, are an accurate reflection of the moral and intellectual health of a community. All these cultural institutions indicate a respect for knowledge, for the truth, for the dignity and worth of the individual—respect of the people for each other and for humanity as a whole. We must beware of any community, and hold its people in contempt of the good opinion of mankind, if it deprives libraries of necessary resources while supporting fully the profit-making activities of questionable enterprises. The hand which bars the library door to knowledge is the hand which stifles the soul of the community.

Bookstores. Bookstore owners are booklovers and friends of all booklovers, dedicated to the interests of readers, young and old. They invest their time and savings in a business from which they hope to derive more of pleasure and fulfillment than of riches. The problems of retail bookselling are complex; the tasks involved require technical training and skill, experience, up-to-date knowledge of books, the ability to get along well with people, and a reasonable amount of business acumen. The bookseller must order his stock of books carefully (usually a few thousand titles selected from lists of perhaps two hundred thousand or more) and arrange them to the best advantage, for he has limited space and must use it for those books which will be especially interesting and helpful to readers. But, of course, he is always willing to order a book not kept in stock if so requested by a serious-minded customer. Patronize your local or nearby bookstores, for they are among the most reliable of the sources of information and centers of culture in American society.

The number of books sold in this country has constantly increased at a faster rate than the population. Annual retail sales of new books amount to nearly 3 billion dollars. In addition, there is a brisk business in the sale of used books and in book collecting. More than 22,000 new titles were published last year (by more than 800 American publishers), besides 8,000 new editions of old books. The new publications covered a wide variety of subjects, arranged according to the number of titles published as follows: economics and sociology (with the largest number of titles); juveniles; science; fiction; religion; literature; technology; medicine; history; education; biography; art; travel; poetry and drama; philosophy and psychology; business; languages; sports and recreation; general reference works; law; home economics; agriculture; and miscellaneous subjects. Including old and new books, more than 80,000 titles (printed in hundreds of millions of copies) are available in low-priced paperbound editions.

There are thousands of regular bookstores (including over 2,000 college bookstores) and, in addition, more than 100,000 stores and stands which display books along with newspapers, magazines, and other merchandise. It is true that millions of people still do not live near a library or bookstore and fail to read books regularly. Nearly everyone reads newspapers and magazines. Daily newspaper circulation is in excess of 61 million copies, while the total annual circulation of magazines is estimated in billions (the circulation of general magazines exceeds 238 million copies per issue). Of course, a single copy of a magazine or a book may be read by dozens of readers. Obviously, the American reader enjoys access to an enormous quantity and range of printed information, much of which is readily available in local or regional libraries, bookstores, and other retail stores.

GOVERNMENTAL, SOCIAL, AND SCIENTIFIC ORGANIZATIONS

Readers can obtain a wide variety of information and useful advice from United States government publications (for a monthly list you can write to the Superintendent of

Documents, Government Printing Office, Washington, D.C. 20402). Research reports, pamphlets, periodicals, and books in all sorts of subject fields are published with a total annual output of more than 60 million copies.

American government publications are respected for their accuracy and objectivity. They are instruments of scholarship useful to all readers, not propaganda tools of any political or ideological group.[1] Many of the publications are printed in large quantities and supplied at little cost to readers. The numerous executive departments of government issue reports on their work, as do the various committees of Congress. Readers can subscribe to the *Congressional Record,* which records in daily issues the proceedings of the House of Representatives and the Senate and includes all votes, speeches, and debates, as well as inserts of political materials. Current lists of new government publications are available in public libraries, and readers can also ask to be placed on the mailing list and deposit funds with the Superintendent of Documents for periodic purchase of pamphlets. Books and pamphlets on child care, home improvements, consumers' problems, gardening, health, science, technology, business, labor, commerce, agriculture, and the arts have been distributed in the millions of copies. Not only do the Department of Defense and the several departments of the armed forces have book libraries containing many millions of copies (for men in the services), but they issue reports and instructional texts printed by the Government Printing Office. Similarly, the Department of Health, Education, and Welfare issues numerous publications, including reports on the researches of the National Institutes of Health and the popular, valuable reports of the United States Office of Education.

Among the innumerable publications of social and scientific organizations most worthy of mention are those

---

[1] An excellent guide to selected government publications, arranged by subject fields, is W. P. Leidy's *A Popular Guide to Government Publications* (Columbia University Press, New York, 1968).

of the American Medical Association, the American Historical Association, the American Sociological Association, the Foreign Policy Association, the National Education Association, the League of Women Voters of the United States, the American Management Association, the Chamber of Commerce of the United States, the National Association of Manufacturers, the American Federation of Labor and the Congress of Industrial Organizations, the Public Affairs Committee, the American Association for the Advancement of Science, the American Library Association, the American Psychological Association, the National Safety Council, the American Standards Association, and the various agencies of the United Nations. Almost every conceivable subject of interest to citizens is represented by some organization and its publications.

SOURCES OF INFORMATION

For most readers, the best single source of information about all book publications in the United States is *Books in Print* (vol. 1, authors; vol. 2, titles), a comprehensive annual guide to all books still in print in the English language. *Books in Print* (published annually by R. W. Bowker Co., New York, N.Y.) is available for consultation in libraries and bookstores. Also available are R. W. Bowker Co.'s *Publishers' Weekly* and *Library Journal,* indispensable journals of book information and news for booksellers and librarians. For readers interested in the names and addresses of publishers of various types of books and magazines, there is a particularly helpful guidebook, a veritable "bible" of the book industry, namely, the *Literary Market Place,* an annual business directory providing information about American and Canadian publishing enterprises.

In the not too distant future, the reader will probably have at his disposal extraordinary new electronic devices which will bring him copies of publications instantaneously. It will then be possible for him to request a book or a portion of any publication by telephone and to be provided with printed copies in his own home at once. Within a few years hence the home library will perhaps contain a million books in microscopic form for immediate selection and magnification. Meanwhile, however, such facilities not being available, readers should certainly make much more frequent and efficient use of those which are on hand, namely, the libraries and bookstores.

SCHOOLS AND UNIVERSITIES

More than 60 million Americans attend some type of school or college and thus constitute a vast audience for the publications discussed above. Books are still the mainstay of instruction in educational institutions on all levels. In thousands upon thousands of day and evening schools and colleges, courses are provided in many hundreds of subjects, cultural, vocational, and social or recreational. With the rise of junior and community colleges, which now exceed 950 in number and enroll about 2 million students, most readers have access to instruction of some kind in fields of interest to them. Highly trained instructors devote special attention to the selection of textbooks and other publications in their subjects and are always pleased to enroll adult students in special groups or at least to provide information about worthwhile books to read. (In addition, about 6 million students are enrolled in home study courses which include many subjects not always available in local schools or colleges.)

Colleges and universities have been experiencing difficult problems owing to their close relationship to contemporary affairs and the revolt of youth against the low standards of activity among leaders of community institutions. The best solution to the problem of higher education is to provide genuine higher education through the serious study of books representing all points of view on controversial matters. Critical, efficient reading is the proper main function of education, and the gap between new and old generations will be closed when both begin to realize that this is indeed the principal business of our schools and colleges. Reading and reasoning are the keys to modern culture and social progress.

READING AND REASONING

Reading requires the reader to understand the logic in an author's ideas and arguments. The reader can usually detect shortcomings and fallacies in printed material if he takes the time to study it carefully. But reading an author's ideas is often only the first proper step in a continuous process of reflection and reaction. What happens after reading—how the reader thinks and feels and what he says and does—determines whether or not the author's work was worth creating and publishing. An author does not write symbols for the purpose of decorating paper; his work is of little value unless it awakens a spark of intellectual life in his readers.

The reader, in effect, begins where the author left off. He digests and absorbs, molds the ideas into the fiber of his own mind. He must be careful to do this correctly, in accordance with the laws of straight thinking. Otherwise, he will only distort the author's material into illogical, confusing, or incorrect conclusions and applications. Efficient reading depends therefore upon straight thinking both during and after the reading experience. The following are a few simple rules of straight thinking.

Rule 1. For straight thinking, the elimination of all prejudice, and I mean *all* prejudice, is absolutely necessary. I recall a brilliant historian who had somehow, as a result of unfortunate experiences, developed a prejudice against Irish Catholics. I could never understand his attitude, for I had myself been happy to associate with Irish Catholics during my childhood and school years and in business, professional, and social enterprises, and had always admired their warmth, sympathy, eloquence, loyalty, and other fine qualities. But he could not read an article or book by anyone named O'Flaherty or O'Brien without at once finding fault. Nearly everything he read by such an author he characterized as part of a plot contrived by the Pope to control the world. How blind are those who will not see the truth! In vain I pointed out that all religious leaders believe their own religion to be the true one, the best, and others to be on the wrong road. Prejudiced readers are totally unable to appreciate the element of truth in social, political, economic, literary, and philosophical views with which they disagree. Thus, unfortunately, the prejudiced reader mistakes his own imperfect vision of the truth for perfection and misses the opportunity to learn from ideas and principles different from his own.

So the first rule of straight thinking is simply to think straight instead of being diverted by prejudice, or more specifically, to follow the author's ideas wherever they lead and to judge them on the basis of his facts and evidence.

Rule 2. Another rule of straight thinking is to assume a position of neutrality when an author's view differs from the popular opinion on any subject. Give him the benefit of the doubt until you consider his facts and evidence. Some readers reject an author's idea immediately because they know or believe that most people do not accept it. This habit is a great mistake. Every reader should consider each idea or proposition on its merits. Sometimes, truth can be popular, but frequently it is very unpopular; in certain historical instances, it has been known to only one man or to only a few men.

Rule 3. The reader should also put aside his emotions when he reads unusual, disturbing ideas or arguments. A person who feels angry or fearful, for example, is not in a good condition to judge another person's ideas justly or correctly. If you are emotionally upset when you read a passage in a newspaper or book, be patient, wait a few days, and reread the same material when you are in a calmer frame of mind. You will then be in a better position to evaluate its message accurately—and discover the truth.

Rule 4. Still another rule of straight thinking tells us that we cannot always depend upon our so-called common sense or even sense perception to find the truth. Things are not universally what they seem to be, for our senses are imperfect and our reasoning powers are limited. So readers should be open-minded about strange ideas presented by any author. How many people fifty years ago would have believed that splitting the atom, which no one could even see, would release vast amounts of energy?

Rule 5. When thinking about an author's ideas, you may obtain fresh insight by turning them inside out or upside down, and then inquiring into the consequences. I have frequently used this technique to good advantage. When I first read about the successful method of nuclear fission, the splitting of atoms, I imagined at once what the opposite process would be, namely, instead of splitting atoms, combining them—the process of fusion. It is probable that many readers thought in the same way. Scientists soon applied high temperatures to create the fusion process of the hydrogen bomb. This reversal of an idea can often lead into new, promising concepts and more useful, and hopefully in the future, morally praiseworthy results.

Rule 6. Finally, the reader should not hesitate to strike out boldly into new paths of imagination during and after his reading. I have had the experience of plunging ahead with new ideas, as in my inventions of instructional materials, testing different arrangements of such materials until I found some that worked effectively. This procedure is not merely trial-and-error thinking, but rather an attempt to organize ideas into a pattern based on a specific goal—for example, to simplify a machine or device or to save time.

6

How To Read Business Contracts And Protect Your Legal Rights

People today often find it necessary to read a variety of legal documents, including contracts to purchase merchandise or real estate, leases, insurance policies, and warranties. These contracts are prepared by specialists who have mastered a technical terminology and language structure protecting their own interests or those of their business clients. But the nonspecialist reader has had little opportunity to become expert in the fine points of such reading materials. Hence he must either employ a specialist to advise him or risk serious misinterpretation and consequent damage to his interests.

Nevertheless, you can learn to read legal documents expertly and derive special advantages from such knowledge and ability. You will then notice at a glance whether or not a particular document is complicated enough to require professional advice. If you employ a specialist, you will better understand the value of his services and will also be in a position to raise questions in case of omissions or forgetfulness on his part. Even attorneys can make mistakes, which an alert reader can sometimes pinpoint. Furthermore, you will be able to remind your adviser about special personal circumstances which might affect the terms or interpretation of a contract or similar legal document. You should not, of course, attempt to be your own lawyer, insurance agent, or product-testing laboratory, but should be prepared to read documents with care and understanding before signing them.

WHAT YOU SHOULD KNOW ABOUT CONTRACTS

Usually some kind of oral or written discussion or negotiation precedes the signing of a contract. The parties may exchange considerable correspondence about the terms and the purpose they have in mind. There might even be a preliminary written agreement to perform certain tasks prior to the signing of a final contract. Any such materials (including memorandums of conversations, with dates and contents threof) should be kept on hand permanently or at least during the life of the contract, for they may have a decisive bearing on the interpretation of some of the terms should controversy come about among the parties.

For example, a troublesome dispute once arose when a business firm sent its contract with a letter stating that the instrument would put into technical form the terms agreed upon in conversations and correspondence with the firm's representative. This statement in the covering letter was incorrect and opened the door to a dispute concerning the meaning and intent of several clauses in the contract. The customer later claimed, and produced letters in support of his claim, that he had never agreed upon what appeared to be specific terms in the signed contract, including especially a clause calling for advance payments for partial performance. A costly lawsuit might well have been avoided if the covering letter had not in effect pointed to the possibility of error or lack of good faith, owing to discrepancies between the contract terms and preceding correspondence.

Legal Advice. If you have had correspondence about the terms of a contract, or if you prepare letters of this kind, show them to your attorney and ask his advice again before signing the contract. What you write in letters may or may not affect the contract, but it could lead to unnecessary disputes. The terms should be spelled out so clearly in the contract itself as not to require further comment or elucidation on your part. Remember, too, that you must not depend on oral modifications or explanations as a means of assuring yourself that the clauses in a contract are accurate and satisfactory.

Sometimes evidence of conversations between the parties can throw light on certain clauses in a faulty contract or can be used to show that the contract is illegal, or that it was signed in error, or that it should be voided as contrary to the laws of a particular state. Notes of these conversations might shed light on the relationships contemplated by the parties, the failure to fulfill conditions on which the enforcement of the contract depends, or subsequent agreements to modify the terms. But courts are reluctant to allow the use of such verbal testimony merely to prove that one of the parties did not mean what the written contract actually states. You should therefore read each clause thoroughly, decide whether it is absolutely correct, consult your attorney, and insist upon the insertion of any necessary change before signing. Minor changes made thereafter will have to be mutually agreed upon and initialled in the margins by the parties, while major changes may make it necessary to supplement or substitute for the original document—in accordance with procedures that will be familiar to your attorney.

Preliminaries. The first statements in a contract identify the parties to the agreement and specify its purpose. This part may be a simple matter, but it is not always so simple as it seems. All parties must be correctly named and identified, their legal addresses should be given, and the date should be filled in as of the day on which the final signature (that of the issuing party) is appended. These details may become important if questions should arise about the terms and performance under the contract.

Parties to a contract should notify each other about changes in their addresses.

Not only the full legal names and addresses, but also the facts of citizenship of the parties should be stated in the contract. Complications may develop if one party is not a citizen. Further, the citizen of one state can sue citizens or firms located in another state either in the state courts or in federal courts as he chooses. Your attorney should make the decisions called for by circumstances of this kind, but it will do no harm to bring them to his attention.

Legal Validity. For a contract to be valid and enforceable, certain conditions must obtain, as follows: (1) there must be a meeting of the minds of the parties to the contract, as to the intent and terms thereof; (2) the agreement must be in writing if the laws of the particular state (in which the contract is made) so provide, but other types of contracts may be oral, although in most cases a detailed written contract is best; (3) the consent of each party must be genuine and voluntary—not induced by mistake, fraud, misrepresentation, undue influence, or compulsion; (4) there must be consideration —that is, something which a party to a contract agrees to do or to refrain from doing in return for the promises, acts, or forbearance by the other party; (5) the parties must be legally competent to enter into the contract (for example, adults can be held to their contract with an infant, but the latter can rescind the contract if he so desires and regain his property); and (6) the agreement must be legal as to its purpose and its performance.

Bear in mind that you will be bound by any contract you sign unless you can prove mistake, fraud, trickery, compulsion, or illegality. Even if you have signed a legal contract without reading it, you will be held responsible for performance in accordance with its terms. An experienced attorney once failed to read his own contract before signing it. I had arranged for a payment to be made to him upon his delivery of one-half of an acceptable manuscript, but he failed to make delivery on time because he had not read the contract. Later he sent more than half of his manuscript and requested payment, which had to be refused because his material was neither acceptable nor delivered on the date specified in the signed contract. This attorney's attorney advised him correctly that he could not make a claim that would be upheld in court. Surely attorneys should know better than to sign contracts without reading them.

If a contract states no date for performance of obligations, each party must perform them within a reasonable time. If, however, the time is specified and is stated to be the essence (the indispensable condition) of the contract, failure of one party to perform on time frees the other party from contractual obligations. If the time element is not of critical importance, failure to perform on time will still be a breach of the contract (subject to suit by the injured party for damage sustained by him as a consequence), but usually it will not give the injured party the right to abandon the entire contract. Unintentional failure to live up to the terms of a contract is no excuse. Each party is held responsible for full performance of his responsibilities at the time and in the manner specified and described in the agreement.

Contracts contain statements of facts and conditions which induce the parties to sign them, and the parties must be able to depend upon the accuracy of these statements. Look for the factual statements, make a list of them, be sure they are accurate, and decide whether any should be changed, deleted, or supplemented. If one party misrepresents or conceals an important fact, the other party may cause the contract to be declared fraudulent and void, and he may sue for damages resulting from the fraud. If both parties make an honest but important mistake on the same matter, either one, if he feels injured by the error, can usually void the contract. If only one party makes an honest mistake, however, he can still be held to the terms of the contract unless the error was obviously known to the other party at the time of his acceptance of the offer.

WHAT TO DO BEFORE SIGNING A CONTRACT

Before signing any contract, read every word and make sure you understand every sentence. Reread every paragraph, noting all facts and obligations. Finally, reread the entire contract and find the answers to the following questions:

1. What statements of fact are included? Which clauses contain these statements?

2. What can either party do if there is a breach of the various terms of the contract by the other party? Which clauses refer to possible failure to perform and the consequences or remedies?

3. Is there a stated time or times for performance? Is time stated to be the essence of the contract? Which clauses specify the time or times for performance?

4. What is the period of the agreement, and how can the contract be terminated?

5. What is said about waivers and changes in the terms of the contract?

6. What is said about the effect of the contract upon heirs, administrators, and executors of any of the parties? About successors and assigns?

Enforcement of Contracts. Consult your attorney immediately if there is doubt as to the correct answers to any of these questions. Do not sign the agreement until you are entirely satisfied with all the statements of facts, conditions, and obligations. Once you have entered into a legal contract, you must expect to live up to all of its terms. Even a state government cannot interfere with enforcement of private contracts. Such interference would deprive citizens of their property illegally under the Fourteenth Amendment to the United States Constitution. Moreover, the Constitution explicitly protects private contracts from violations by the states. Section 10 of

Article 1 provides that no state shall pass any law "impairing the obligations of contracts," and even in an emergency a state can only delay execution of contracts for the public welfare a reasonable time while conserving fully the interests of all parties thereto.

Complexity of Contracts. Obviously, contract law is highly complex. It is usually necessary to consult an attorney because contracts today are not based on a single, simple idea, such as the idea that men should always keep their promises, or the idea that they should be compelled to live up to a bargain once made, or the idea that they should not give up something they own without receiving equal value in return. Simple ideas of this kind just do not work well in modern business. Talk is cheap, for instance, and many promises do not have to be kept so far as the law is concerned. Bargains made can be illegal or ambiguous. Anyone should be free to give up his property without an equal return if he so chooses. Our contract laws are a complicated mixture based partly on these ideas, but also upon state and federal laws, established business customs, and numerous court decisions. On many points the legal experts themselves disagree. So there is no way out of the dilemma. You must read your contracts carefully, consult a conscientious, reputable attorney, and try to transact your business with people whom you can trust.

It is easy to read a contract quickly and assume that everything is quite satisfactory and in order, but that can be a dangerous assumption. The following examples indicate only a few of the problems which can arise in this complicated business. Even if these particular examples may not apply to your immediate situation, they will remind you of important points to consider whenever you contemplate signing a contract of any kind.

1. Apartment leases are contracts which usually provide for some means of terminating the lease. In leases extending for a definite period of time, the last day of tenancy is always stated, but thereafter the tenant can continue as a month-to-month tenant with the consent of

the landlord. For a lease of one year or longer, the land-lord can in many cases choose between extending the lease another full year or dispossessing the tenant hold-over. In some leases, a renewal clause provides that the tenant must notify the landlord (within a stipulated period) of his intention to vacate the premises, and often there is a clause stating that the lease will be automatically renewed unless the tenant so notifies the landlord. (Of course, you can agree with your landlord either orally or in writing to terminate the lease at any time before the final date.)

Most of the standard printed leases tend to protect the interests of the landlord. They specify, for example, that he can evict the tenant for non-payment of rent or of certain expenses for upkeep if these are stated in the lease. As a tenant, however, you should know that you, too, have rights under the law of *constructive eviction*. Thus, you can move out and sue for damages if the landlord fails to furnish services agreed upon, such as heat, conceals a dangerous condition, or allows the premises to be infested with pests or to become uninhabitable in part or in whole. So read your lease from beginning to end and ask your attorney's advice before signing it.

2. Sometimes a contract may be so worded as to grant you rights and privileges of which you may not be fully aware. Be sure to inquire about such possibilities when you consult your attorney. For example, contracts between authors and publishers usually stipulate that "without the written consent of the Publisher . . . the author shall not write, edit, print or publish . . . any other literary work of so similar a character that it would be liable to compete or interfere with or injure the sale" of the author's book.

How often authors have assumed that such a clause prevents them from writing another book for a different publisher on the same subject! In most instances they are perfectly free to write additional books on the same subject, provided that the new books are larger works priced so much higher than their first book that there would be no competition between them. Certainly journal articles would ordinarily not compete with their book, but rather would help the sale. The key words in the contract are "liable to compete or interfere with or injure the sale," as applied to the original book. Obviously, it would not be fair to expect the publisher to invest heavily in an author's work and then allow the author to publish a directly competing work with another publisher.

3. You can sometimes arrange for modification of your contract by mutual agreement. Contracts generally include a clause stating that "no waiver of any breach of any term or condition of this Agreement shall be binding unless the same is in writing and signed by the party waiving such breach . . . No provision of this Agreement may be changed except by an instrument in writing signed by the parties." According to this clause, if one party fails to fulfill a specified obligation under the contract, it is still possible for the other party to eliminate the obligation by signing a written statement to this effect. That statement actually changes one of the terms of the contract and should therefore be signed by both parties. Such a change will not then injure or destroy the contract or modify it in any other respect.

4. An automobile liability insurance contract protects you against claims by other people for injury to them or damage to their property. Read your contract carefully and consult your agent immediately in case of accident. To collect damages from your insurance company, a claimant must theoretically prove that you were negligent and that he did not contribute to the accident through his own negligence. It has become the custom with most insurance companies, however, to pay moderate claims instead of going to the expense of a lawsuit. They seem to be quite willing to pay claims against you in accordance with the contract, but remember that they will probably raise your annual premium and the increase will continue for several years. It will therefore be a costly experience. Many automobile owners have preferred to pay small claims themselves, even when they

are not at fault. They keep their accident policy in force as a means of protection in the less likely event of serious or fatal accidents. The injustice of the present system, with its bickering, confusion, long delays in litigation, costly expenses for lawyers' services, and opportunity for chicanery, has become so apparent that the public is demanding a new system of liability insurance (comparable to the best types of fire insurance) which would ignore the question of negligence or blame and compensate the victim for his actual injury or property damage.

Troubles with contracts occur because the average person has neither the time nor the resources to compete with business organizations which can afford to employ batteries of attorneys throughout the year to construct, interpret, and enforce their complicated contracts. If you sign a homeowners' insurance policy, for example, the total cost of the insurance might be only a few hundred dollars over a period of several years. You would not employ an expert attorney for a period of six months to study your contract or to protect your interests. Your attorney may give you a half-hour for consultation, but he starts at a disadvantage. A large insurance firm has prepared the same contract for thousands, possibly hundreds of thousands, of individual policyholders. It can afford to hire the best talent in the legal profession for careful preparation and interpretation of the contract so as to protect the company against high risks and bring in the maximum profit.

Among the most objectionable of the complex contracts are some in the field of installment purchases. These contracts may include clauses whereby the debtor gives up his right to question the justice of the debt even if he later discovers that he has been victimized; or clauses which allow the lender (seller) to sell the credit contract to a finance company which can then collect payments from the customer even if the seller has defrauded him by delivering defective merchandise. Several organizations, including the Consumer Federation of America and the American Federation of Labor and Congress of Industrial

Organizations, have been active in condemning such unjust contracts. But why have not the business associations of this country taken appropriate action to protect consumers? One can only conclude that higher and higher profits take precedence over the ideals of fair play and public welfare, a shortsighted policy of neglect which can only severely damage the long-term interests of business. You must therefore study any such contract carefully and obtain competent legal advice before signing it. Very few of the states have enacted adequate legislation to protect the consumer from abuses perpetrated by means of these ingenious contracts. Unfortunately, there seems to be no substitute for stringent federal laws to protect the average citizen, together with full publicity about conditions by organizations representing the consumer, and certainly no substitute for the rule that every citizen should become an alert, critical reader of contracts.

On the other hand, there are many business managers of high integrity who strive to be fair and honest in their contractual relationships. In the publishing industry, reputable firms have developed satisfactory contracts, based upon decades of experience, which protect fully the interests of the author as well as those of the publisher. But I have seen contracts of certain publishers which were ingeniously drawn in such a way as to make it highly improbable that justice could ever be done to their authors. In some contracts, ambiguous terms are included, as well as obligations of the author to pay costs which he could not possibly anticipate or verify. I have seen a contract which actually ties the authors down to the publisher in such a manner as to prevent them from ever escaping his clutches. In the publishing industry there is an authors' association which has begun to advise authors about these troublesome contracts. In most business transactions, however, the millions of American consumers have no organization to analyze and protect their individual contractual interests. Consequently, it will become increasingly necessary in these vital matters for elected representatives in the state and federal governments to intervene and represent the people who elected them. In addition, a consumers' legal research association is urgently needed, an organization which would do nothing else but study and publicize contract practices from the point of view of the virtually defenseless individual citizen.

THE LANGUAGE IN CONTRACTS

Most of the words in printed contracts are familiar to readers and give them little difficulty, but there are a few words with special meanings and these can be so confusing or disturbing to a reader that he is tempted to sign the contract without fully understanding all the clauses. Be sure to ask your attorney to explain the meaning of any terms in your contract which you do not understand.

The following terms are used frequently in many types of contracts. The explanations may be quite helpful during your negotiations and reading of a contract. By learning the precise meanings of these terms you will not have to waste your attorney's time on them.

acquittal, or acquittance. A release or discharge of a party from a contract obligation.

affidavit. A written, sworn statement.

affidavit of title. In the sale of real estate, a written statement made by the seller under oath, attesting to the identity of the owner of record, his lack of knowledge concerning unrecorded encumbrances or ownership claims by others, his marital status if he and his wife execute the deed, and his assurance that there are no unrecorded judgments against him.

arbitration. In disputes as to the terms of a contract, a method of settlement by submitting the matter to mutually agreed upon persons for their decision or award.

assignment. The transfer of contract rights and obligations by one person (the assignor) to another (the assignee) who becomes a new party to the original contract.

chattel mortgage. A mortgage on articles of personal property, movable or immovable, as distinguished from real estate or things which are considered to be part and parcel of real estate.

closing of title. The transfer of title to property through the delivery of a deed by the seller to the buyer.

consideration. Something given up by one party to a contract, or something he agrees to do or to refrain from doing, in return for the promises, acts, or forbearances of the other party.

contract under seal. A contract which contains a signatory's symbol in the form of a seal, such as a wax impression, scroll, or other symbol.

conveyance of title. An instrument (such as a deed) or method for transferring one's title to and interest in real estate or one's property rights to another person.

covenant. A legally valid, enforceable agreement, undertaking, or promise. In a covenant deed, the grantor affirms stated facts and conditions and agrees that, in case of dispute, he will uphold the grantee's title and his right to use the transferred property.

coverage. The total amount of risk assumed by an insurance company, including all its liabilities for payments to the insured in case of eventualities stated in an insurance contract.

deductible. An amount, specified in an insurance contract, which the insurance company deducts from the total payment that would otherwise be due to the insured under the terms of his contract.

deed. A written instrument under seal conveying title to and rights to the use of real estate from a seller (or grantor) to a buyer (or grantee).

default. Failure to fulfill or obey the terms of a contract. Failure to appear in court proceedings on time may cause a party to lose his case by default.

demised premises. Premises entrusted to a person for his use in accordance with the terms of a lease, implying his right to quiet enjoyment of the premises.

easement. The right of a person, either as set forth in

a written contract or as otherwise acquired or allowed by law, to use the land of another person for stated purposes.

encumbrance. A lien or claim against the property of one person by another.

fee simple. Lifelong, inheritable, unrestricted ownership of real estate property, including the right to keep, use, and dispose of it, subject only to regulations imposed by law.

fiduciary. A person acting in the capacity of trustee, i.e., holding property in trust for another person and obligated to conserve his interest therein.

full covenant and warranty deed. A deed for the conveyance of real estate property whereby the grantor guarantees the accuracy of facts and conditions stated therein—including his ownership and right to transfer it, and the absence of any encumbrances—and agrees to provide any evidences needed to perfect the title or to guarantee the title in perpetuity.

indenture. An official or formal document, such as a deed or a written contract, which sets forth the facts, conditions, promises, acts, and terms agreed upon by the parties.

infringement. Any breach or violation of the terms of an agreement, or any trespass by one person against the rights or privileges of another person.

larceny. In insurance contracts, the unlawful removal of personal goods without the consent of the rightful owner and with the intent either to deprive the owner of their use or to use them for the thief's own purposes.

lien. A claim, charge, or encumbrance against property, real or personal, based upon the owner's debt or obligation to the person holding or legally entitled to the lien.

limit of liability. In insurance contracts, the maximum amount which the insurance company is obligated to pay as compensation to or in behalf of the insured.

merger. In real estate law, when one person has two rights, one broader or more important than the other, the narrow right is destroyed by being merged, or absorbed, into the broad one. Thus, if a tenant has a lease but later becomes owner of the same property, his rights as a tenant disappear because they have been merged into his broader rights as the owner.

obligee. In business contracts, a person who is entitled to payments or other benefits to be derived from the other party's performance of a specified obligation.

obligor. In business contracts, a person who has agreed to perform (or to refrain from performing) a stated act or to make specified payments.

pilferage. In insurance contracts, the illegal appropriation of small amounts of money or articles of little value without the owner's consent.

quitclaim deed. A deed whereby the grantor surrenders any of his own interest in or ownership claims to property described therein, but without giving the grantee any guarantee or warranty of title.

robbery. In insurance contracts, the unlawful taking and removing of personal property from an owner usually by violence or threat of injury.

stipulations. Specific conditions and terms stated in a contract. In court cases, facts or evidence mutually agreed upon by opposing attorneys.

successor in title. The person who takes over the title to real estate property from a previous owner.

summary dispossess proceedings. In real estate contracts, a procedure whereby a landlord petitions a court to order a tenant to vacate the owner's premises for non-payment of rent or other stated reasons, the tenant either appears to oppose the petition or fails to appear, and the court makes the decision to issue or not to issue a warrant of dispossess. If the warrant is issued, it may be delayed for a reasonable time by the court, after which the tenant can be forcibly removed by a marshal.

survival clause. In real estate transactions, a special clause in the contract of sale which keeps a stated provision or obligation in force after the delivery of the deed;

in the absence of such a clause, the contract of sale is destroyed by being merged into the deed.

theft. Identical with larceny, except that theft is sometimes defined to include not only unlawful appropriation or swindling, but also the act of obtaining possession of another's personal goods legally and then later misusing them for the thief's own purposes. Insurance policies use both terms (theft and larceny) to make certain that all such acts are included.

trustee. A person who holds property in trust for the benefit of another person and has legal title thereto until the purposes of the trust have been carried out.

waiver. A contract clause or a written instrument whereby a person agrees to surrender stated legal rights. Sometimes the acts of a person may indicate that he intends to waive (abandon) certain contractual or legal rights.

warrant. This term means to guarantee that specified facts and conditions are true.

7

How To Appreciate
Literature And Enjoy Your Reading

The enjoyment of literature begins with attentive, thoughtful interpretation of the author's purpose, design, and message. The reader cannot derive true understanding and enjoyment through superficial or careless reading, which is, in fact, the principal obstacle to the appreciation of literature. He must keep his eyes and mind open and alert to the author's language, pausing now and then to think and rethink what has been read and to ask, "What was particularly pleasing, unusual, effective, or significant in such passages?"

Thoughtful Review. You should review and recall the material you have read in any magazine or book and thus take pleasure again, perhaps more deeply than before, in its ideas and presentation. The experience of rethinking what you read is comparable to the pleasant recollection of tasty food you have eaten with relish, a source of repeated satisfaction and delight.

Elimination of Irrelevancies. Do your best to ignore jarring or unpleasant aspects of reading material. On occasion, rough expressions and horrifying incidents are natural or even essential ingredients of literature, depicting realities and truths. However, smut inserted gratuitously and artificially creates an obnoxious obstacle to reading enjoyment, revealing lack of taste on the part of the author or perhaps excessive zeal to attract and enlarge his reading audience. The sensitive reader's enjoyment is blunted and sometimes ruined by these annoying irrelevancies, just as the enjoyment of a fine dinner can be disturbed by unclean silver or a soiled tablecloth. There is no excuse for intruding bodily functions unnecessarily or excessively into literary work which should appeal to the deepest understanding and highest aspirations and loftiest sentiments—the great concerns and interests—of mankind. For the maximum enjoyment of reading, concentrate upon the effective, convincing, natural, significant, outstanding elements, applying to each passage and work as a whole a sense of alert discrimination and appreciation.

Critical Evaluation. Search out, recognize, and admire the special skills of the author, his choice of apt, vivid language, variety of style, lively rhythm, striking characterization, and his use of suspense, implication, exaggeration, understatement, irony, and other techniques. As you read, take note of these special qualities which lend power and eloquence to the language, and as you recall what you have read, anticipate more of the same enjoyment from what you are about to read.

Sharing of Experience. We understand, appreciate, and enjoy most of all the experiences which we share with others. Readers should pause frequently in their reading to express their innermost thoughts and feelings about the author's work. Often it is helpful to predict events, ideas, or moods in sections you are about to read, just as you anticipate events in real life, even though things may not always turn out precisely as expected. There is satisfaction when one's expectations are realized, but also when one is pleasantly surprised by unanticipated events.

ASPECTS OF LITERARY APPRECIATION

There are five main aspects or qualities of literature, which may be described as architectural, pictorial, musical, philosophical, and psychological, owing to the resemblance of the literary art to these other forms of creative expression or experience.

The Architectural Aspect. The architectural aspect of literature refers to the overall design of a literary work, to the elements of balance and harmony prevailing among its parts, and to the unification of these elements so that the work as a whole appeals to the reading audience as a significant experience. When we view with wonder and awe masterpieces of our architectural heritage—such as the Gothic cathedrals of Europe, with their soaring arches, delicate vaults, and spires reaching to the sky, their grotesque statues and decorations, and their brilliant stained glass windows—we see unification through design, color, and ornament. Literature, too, must possess a unified structure, a joining of harmonious parts. Although the reader need not attempt detailed analysis during his reading, he should observe the overall plan, because an awareness of the work as a whole will illuminate each of its parts. Often a preview of the author's plan, by rapid skimming, will clarify separate passages and link them in a meaningful, symmetrical structure. Thus the reader fits each part at once into the skeleton on which the author has built linguistic flesh and blood.

The structural framework of a literary work links the main and subordinate themes. The reader naturally is eager to know what the author had in mind, what his principal message or idea consists of, how the first section introduces the next, how the early parts lead to the main points or climaxes, and how the flow of words and ideas, whether continuous or reminiscent, is brought to a fitting, satisfying close. For most readers, it is enough to note the design and arrangement employed by the author and to bear them in mind as they concentrate on each part in turn. In this way they will more clearly grasp the significance of the author's ideas, language, themes, moods, and implications. Reading separate parts without a view of the whole is comparable to visiting a once inspiring or beautiful edifice now bereft of walls and roof—no longer a thing of beauty but a ruin until repaired and skillfully restored.

Pictorial Aspect. The pictorial aspect of literature corresponds to an artist's work which fills in and gives body to his overall design—the sensitive, graceful lines and forms, delicate or sparkling colors, shadows, and contrasts, backgrounds, orderly arrangements, and picturesque effects which are to be found in art. In literature, comparable details fill in the design and impart distinctive qualities to a poem, story, play, or essay—a fresh or unusual setting, unique characters, significant expressions and central motifs, the flesh and bones that fit into the author's framework and give substance to his work. The reader needs to ask again and again as he reads, *What is distinctive about this part, unusual or striking, natural or surprising, particularly convincing and effective?* Such questions, by helping him enlarge the scope of his attention and notice what might otherwise be lost to him, effectively broaden and deepen his appreciation and enjoyment of literature.

Pictorial effects in poetry and prose may be either specific or merely implied. The author uses familiar words in new ways and arrangements to produce these effects. In art, a painting such as the Mona Lisa will possess striking natural, lifelike form and coloring, and, at the same time, that imaginative quality of vague suggestibility represented by the variant tones and graceful smiling lips of the mysterious lady as depicted by Leonardo da Vinci. Picasso, like an author using familiar words, starts with commonplace objects but adds his own vision as he creates, to form significant, powerfully suggestive works, combining classical with modern, that are subject to widely different interpretations. In literature, too, interpretations of meaning will differ widely with readers; painter and author both intermingle clear and simple ideas with impressions.

If literature is abstracted, digested, abridged, or compressed excessively by editors, the original work may be seriously mutilated, and the reader of such versions will receive a distorted impression, just as if masses of color were detached from a painting. With links and joints gone, the body of the work becomes merely a trunk without head or limbs. Authors, like painters, should never permit mutilation of their work. Readers should notice and appreciate the significance of the large, central themes, but see them as parts of the whole, not as if detached from the author's overall plan.

Similarly, if the flow of literature is interrupted with too many explanations or discussions, as in certain educational methods which dissect unnecessarily, the author's art may be destroyed, thus stimulating distaste instead of enthusiasm for creative masterpieces. Therefore, when you read, give your attention wholeheartedly to the author's design and postpone serious analysis and investigation, excepting a minimum of information or allusions required for understanding the main themes of the work.

Musical Aspect. Literature has musical qualities that are created by sound, rhythm, repetition and rhyme, phrasing, length and variety of words, pauses, and the flow of, and linkage between, main and subordinate themes. The author selects words to express a mood or a motif; his message may be stated directly or by implication. Just as the abrupt, descending, glissando notes of music may remind one of a waterfall, so do the author's choice of words and their arrangement reflect the meaning of his theme. Thus, Iago's drinking song, sung to the clinking of wineglasses, in Shakespeare's *Othello*, applies sound, rhyme, repetition, and emphasis:

> And let me the canakin clink, clink!
> And let me the canakin clink!
> A soldier's a man;
> A life's but a span:
> Why, then, let a soldier drink.
>   (Act II, Scene iii)

The words almost make their own music, as the reader imagines the voice and glasses producing these sounds. Alert readers enjoy such musical qualities as they journey along the heights and valleys of the author's landscape, a creative adventure reflecting his plan, vision, and skill.

Philosophical Aspect. The philosophical aspect of literature offers the discerning reader models of clear thinking, logical ideas, and rational meanings. He asks, *What do these passages signify as to truth, reality, insight into nature and the nature of man? How do the author and his characters interpret the values of life?* The thoughtful reader will agree, disagree or suspend judgment.

An author's philosophy of life can be expressed directly in a few lines, as in Walt Whitman's notes:

> After you have exhausted what there is in business, politics, conviviality, love, and so on—have found that none of these finally satisfy, or permanently wear— what remains? Nature remains; to bring out from their torpid recesses, the affinities of a man or woman with the open air, the trees, fields, the changes of seasons— the sun by day and the stars of heaven by night.

Or the ideas of a particular society, historical period, or individual may be developed gradually in the plot, the dialogue, or the commentaries. Often the author's personal views are unknown, for he may present characters adhering to diverse philosophies of life without taking sides. The reader must ponder and appreciate explicit or implied values, moral or spiritual standards and insights, encountered in his reading.

Psychological Aspects. Finally, and most importantly, the author and his readers participate in a joint psychological enterprise. Even though his own philosophy of life may not be revealed, something of the author's personality and spirit shows itself in his language, characters, and themes. Only a sensitive, imaginative person can create a literary masterpiece. Further, the characters in a play or novel speak and act in ways which grow out of their inner thoughts or feelings. They may expand or deteriorate psychologically, display emotions and motives or conceal them, behave in or out of character, and it is a task and challenge for the reader to appreciate all such characteristics. It is indeed the reader's task to speak with the speakers, think with the thinkers, feel with the characters—in other words, at least for the time being, identify himself psychologically with the ideas, purposes, emotions, and spirit infusing the work. For the fullest appreciation and enjoyment of literature, the reader must momentarily feel as the villain feels, as the hero feels, as the author feels, despite reservations or revulsion which may afterward impel him to reject any and all.

ENJOYMENT OF POETRY

If you noticed the sadness of a lonely friend, perhaps you would wonder in commonplace language, "What is wrong? My friend is out of sorts today." The following stanza of a poem by the sixteenth-century poet Thomas Wyatt expresses his reactions to the sadness of a friend:

> Her pains tormented me so sore
> That comfort had I none,
> But cursed my fortune more and more
> To see her sob and groan:
> Alas the while!

Wyatt's lines provide a clue to the chief differences between poetry and prose. *First*, the word order in his poem differs from the usual order in prose, thus lending greater force and power. *Second*, the words are arranged in a rhythmic pattern (and include rhyme) with stress on the same words, use of alternately short and long syllables, and corresponding breath control, as in oral reading or speech. Wyatt's poem should be read aloud. *Third*, the language is extremely intense, compressed, and highly emotional, expressing deep feelings through the intimate union of sound and meaning, that is to say, through the use of words which, when spoken, will impart emphasis and power to the author's intended mood and idea. (The short emphatic words and repetition of the consonant *s* in Wyatt's stanza illustrate this effect.)

Finally, the overall theme and effect are much more dramatic than is customary in prose—comparable, in fact, to the dramatic themes and effects of words and music in grand opera. The best of prose writings may bear some resemblance to the rhythms and other imagination-stirring characteristics of poetry, but poems exhibit in greater measure the qualities of word power, rhythm, emphasis, emotion, and dramatic implication. They possess a unique depth and beauty of expression, inspiring and fascinating the sensitive reader. Their essence flows from these unique qualities in which the details of information, explicit ideas, and events, so important in prose, are subordinated. The dominance of rhythmic sound (sometimes including rhyme), unusual order and emphases, and dramatic or ultra-sensitive moods reflecting the poet's attitude make poetry the most musical and emotionally stirring of literary forms.

Rhythm and Rhyme. The rhythm and rhyme of poetry are powerful aids to memory. We can long remember words of a poem because they are arranged in regular groupings connected by means of the same or similar repeated sounds. Poetry may have originated in ancient times as ballads sung to report events people wanted to remember. The rhymes of the ballads made recall much easier. Moreover, the earliest peoples depended upon speech and song for their information. Most of them could neither write nor read, but all could speak and sing.

As a child I lived in a poorly constructed wooden house with an upstairs neighbor partial to liquor who resented what he regarded as excessive rents. He was a sturdy fellow and one day, under the influence, doubled up his fists and smashed them through the flimsy boards of the hallway. Ordinarily I would have forgotten the incident, for drunkenness and violence were as common then as they are today. But I composed a ditty about the event and to this day, sixty years afterward, both the circumstances and the silly doggerel verse remain vivid in my memory:

> The landlord said to the tenant,
> "I've come for the rent."
> The tenant said,
> "I will not pay the rent."
> The landlord went away,
> And the tenant said,
> "In the hall I'll make a dent."
> So he made a hole
> In the wall of the hall.
>
> The landlord came and asked,
> "When will you pay the rent?"
> The tenant answered, "Never.
> Look at the dent.
> Look at the hole
> In the wall of the hall."
> The landlord hit the tenant
> And the tenant hit the landlord.
> Each hit the other gent.
>
> Moral for landlords:
> Never ask for the rent.

Indeed, the reader can best remember and enjoy poems by noting their regular pattern and sounds and by relating them to his own experience.

The words in a line of poetry possess much more rhythm and more regular patterns than those in a prose sentence. Noting the rhythmic patterns used in a poem can often make it easier to read, understand, remember, and enjoy. Sometimes, unless you recognize the pattern, you can misread the poet's meaning and intention.

The most common pattern is the iambic, in which there is stress on the second of each pair of syllables. The following example is from Coleridge's *The Rime of the Ancient Mariner:*

> He wént like óne that háth been stúnned,
> And ís of sénse forlórn:
> A sádder ánd a wíser man
> He róse the mórrow mórn.

In prose, the same ideas would be expressed in sentences lacking such regular meter and rhyme, as, for example:

"He walked around like someone in a state of shock, deprived of his senses, but when he got up the next morning, he was a sadder and wiser man." Poetry depends upon a more or less regular rhythmic arrangement of words for its special images and moods, but the lines must not become too monotonous. A certain amount of irregularity must therefore be introduced:

> Sweetly, sweetly blew the breeze—
> On me alone it blew.

Here Coleridge has avoided monotony by using trochaic meter in the first line (stressing the first of two syllables) and iambic meter in the second line. (A stressed syllable tends to be held a little longer than an unstressed one.) The mixture of rhythmic forms can be so irregular that there is little uniformity of rhythm, no rigid pattern of meter, from one line to the next, as in free verse:

I think I could turn and live with animals, they are so placid
    and self-contained;
I stand and look at them long and long.
They do not stand and whine about their condition;
They do not lie awake in the dark and weep for their sins; . . .

Here the free verse of Walt Whitman in *The Beasts* comes close to the rhythm of speech, yet retains a certain repetitive sameness among some of the phrases and lines to make them more convincing and emphatic than ordinary conversation.

Among the most common metric patterns are the following:

He práyeth wéll, who lóveth wéll   (iambus) (iambic tetrameter)
Both mán and bírd and beást.

Swíftly, swíftly fléw the ship   (trochee) (trochaic tetrameter)
Yet shé sailed sóftly tóo: (iambus) (iambic trimeter)
We can líve without boóks,   (anapest) (anapestic dimeter)
We can't líve without coóks.

When I pláy on my fíddle   (anapest) (anapestic trimeter)
  in Doóney,
Folk dançe like a wave of
  the séa;

Oń to the boúnd of the   (dactyl) (dactylic trimeter)
  waśte,
Oń, to the Cíty of Gód.

Lísten to mé and obéy: (dactyl) (dactylic trimeter)
Ońe, twó, thŕee, fóur,   (spondee) (spondaic tetrameter)
Knóck at the doór.   (dactyl) (dactylic dimeter)
Twó, foúr, síx, eíght;   (spondee) (spondaic tetrameter)
Wáit at the gáte.   (dactyl) (dactylic dimeter)

I spráng to the stírrup, and   (amphibrach, tetrameter)
  Jóris, and hé;
I gálloped, Dirćk gálloped,
  we gálloped all thŕee;

Just as doctors and lawyers use a technical language (derived in part from Latin) which ohly confuses their clients, so the critics and teachers of literature use technical words which annoy readers interested in learning more about poetry. A line of poetry is divided into feet, each consisting of stressed (or strong) and unstressed (or weak) syllables. If a line has five feet, each made up of one weak syllable followed by one strong syllable, why not call it a weak-strong five-foot line, instead of using the technical term, *iambic pentameter*? Technical language can be saved for the advanced students or specialists, although many of them, too, might join the majority of readers who prefer ordinary English. Thus, *iambic trimeter* could be known as weak-strong three-foot lines; *anapestic dimeter*, as weak-weak-strong two-foot lines; and *dactyllic hexameter*, as strong-weak-weak six-foot lines.

Some contemporary poets intermingle various rhythmic patterns, using pauses, swift changes of pace, alliteration, analogy, metaphors, figures of speech, and omissions of expected words to express vivid emotions and images. They create lyric poetry, short, personal, intensely emotional poems, the most musical of literary forms, particularly effective when read aloud with emphasis and intonation pattern attuned to the poet's mood or message. Few poets attempt to create narrative poems built around the story element as a central core, or to emulate the long, heroic narratives or the classical epics, the historical accounts dramatized by means of steady metrical patterns and powerful rhythms of majestic, dignified language. Modern poetry depends upon its capacity to suggest moods and meanings, impressions, inexpressible truths.

Repetition of a single poem can be overdone, just as in prose excessive use of an expression makes it stale, a cliché. Similarly, in music, we can enjoy a melody repeated a few times, but cannot endure excessive repetition. It is best to read a wide variety of poems, although we may never weary of memorable works recited at reasonably frequent intervals if we can divine new, fresh meanings in them.

Translations. Poetry has been recited or written abundantly in hundreds of languages. All emotions are expressible in any language, even though a particular language may seem to have a structure more effective in expressing one kind of feeling than another. (In my own subjective experience with poetry in languages other than my native, superbly eloquent English, I have felt poetry in Hebrew to be uniquely dignified and dramatic, that in Latin to be most heroic and emphatic, that in Russian to be strongly measured, deeply moving, and intense, that in German to be extremely sensitive and affecting, that in French to be most thoughtful and inspiring, that in Italian to be the most musical and emotional.) There is no adequate substitute for reading the original poem in the author's native language. True, an approximate notion of theme, action, or mood can often be duplicated by a skilled translator, yet even the best will come short of the original, sometimes distorting it, failing to reproduce its true meaning. Indeed, as the gifted poet and discerning interpreter of poetry, Stanley Burnshaw, has pointed out in his significant book, *The Poem Itself,* "Regardless of its brilliance, an English translation is always a different thing; it is always an *English poem* . . ." and each individual word in a poem is "a unique totality—unique in sound, denotation, connotation, and doubtless much more." [1]

To appreciate every aspect of a poem—architectural, pictorial, musical, philosophical, and psychological—you must become familiar with its original language, and also with its related people and culture, the native speakers and writers, to capture all its nuances, moods, emphases, rhythms, and implications. A translation may be all you have for the moment, yet it is only a pointer to the original, just as a sensitive painter's rough, preliminary sketch gives only a hint of his final masterpiece. Most often in fact, it is better to learn enough of another language to read its poetry and catch the spirit of the poet and his people than it would be to read only the translations. Examine two or three translations of a classic; they may differ so widely that you will wonder whether they are translations of the same original. To appreciate and enjoy poetry created in a foreign language, it is necessary to learn the basic essentials of the language and then to read the original together with the best available translations and commentaries.

ENJOYMENT OF PLAYS

Some readers avoid plays, even the works of Shakespeare, often because an uninspired teacher in the past has dissected the plots and language into tidbits or absurdities which distorted the architectural grandeur,

---

[1] Stanley Burnshaw, *The Poem Itself* (New York: Holt, Rinehart & Winston, 1960; paperbound edition, Schocken Books, Inc., 1967), p. xii. See also Stanley Burnshaw's illuminating discussion of this point in his *The Seamless Web* (New York: George Braziller, Inc., 1970), pp. 209–212; and his comments (using Thomas Mann's *Tonio Kröger* as an example) on translation of prose writings in his *Varieties of Literary Expression* (New York: New York University Press, 1962).

language, and emotional impact of each work. Reading a play should be almost the same as observing the identical things being said and done in life situations by real people corresponding precisely in every respect—costume, appearance, speech, motives, capacities, virtues, and failings—to the characters in the play. The reader should read a play, not through the eyes of a teacher or a critic, but through his own eyes and ears, reading aloud, as if he were a spectator of the events, or at least part of a theater audience. In this way the playwright's true design and intent, his aggregation of things done, said, and seen, will inspire a sympathetic understanding and response in the reader's mind and heart. Later, but only later, he may enrich and deepen his insight, preferably after attending a performance of the play itself. Then, not before, is the time for guidebooks, lectures, and readings of commentaries or dramatic histories.

The Play Itself. So, I say, "To the works themselves!" Read and reread them, just as you look again and again at a beautiful painting by Raphael or listen again and again to a Beethoven symphony—and there will be time thereafter for discussion, dissection, and interpretation. Do not ruin the immediate experience by suffering interruptions with bits of humdrum remarks, but give your attention to each work as a whole in its master's dress.

Beware of truncated versions of plays. Abridgment of a play to fit it into an hour's time instead of three can distort the work. The overemphasis on one or more of its parts, the lack of unified appreciation, the separation of meanings which should be joined like inseparable twins—these are the means used by overspecialized critics to spoil the best of dramatic literature by bringing it down to the level of commonplace, amateurish conceptions. It is no wonder that many readers learn mainly distaste for the best of drama, as well as poetry and prose. So I say, again, "To the works themselves!"

Use of the Imagination. What do we in our imagination see, hear, and feel when we read a play such as Shakespeare's tragedy, *Macbeth*? Consider the opening scene of Act I.

We see before us a desolate bare plot of land swept by a violent thunderstorm. Suddenly the dim, grotesque figures of three old witches appear out of nowhere. We picture them as bent-over hags in black, with pointed noses and long, sharp nails. We hear their harsh voices croaking:

> When shall we three meet again in stormy weather?
> Before the sun sets.
> Where?
> Upon the heath.
> To meet Macbeth.

As we watch and listen tensely, we sense that something is wrong, out of joint, and we feel trouble coming as the three old hags screech together their chant that their world is an evil one, upside down—that what is good for people is foul to witches:

> Fair is foul, and foul is fair.
> Hover through the fog and filthy air.

And they melt away into the windstorm. Now we know that we must expect trouble ahead and that Macbeth, a general in the king's army, will be in it.

Let us go on to the second scene of Act I and imagine ourselves at the military headquarters of Duncan, King of Scotland. We see the King and his two sons strolling on the camp grounds with the Scot nobleman Lennox and a few servants when there is shouting nearby and a sergeant stumbles before them bleeding from his battle wounds. We hear the King ask, "Who is this bleeding soldier? Perhaps he can tell us what has happened in the battle of the rebels against my authority."

> What bloody man is that? He can report,
> As seemeth by his plight, of the revolt
> The newest state.

The King's son recognizes the wounded sergeant as a brave soldier who had helped to rescue him in battle, and urges him to speak up:

> This is the sergeant
> Who like a good and hardy soldier fought
> 'Gainst my captivity. Hail, brave friend!
> Say to the king the knowledge of the broil
> As thou didst leave it.

We hear the sergeant explain that the rebels had been winning in the desperate battle until Macbeth rushed forward recklessly, swinging his hot sword of steel, killed many of the enemy, and finally ripped their leader in two from his navel to the jaw and strung him up on a wall. We notice the wounded soldier's sincere admiration for Macbeth's courage:

> For brave Macbeth—well he deserves that name—
> Disdaining fortune, with his brandish'd steel,
> Which smoked with bloody execution,
> Like valour's minion carved out his passage
> Till he faced the slave;
> Which ne'er shook hands nor bade farewell to him,
> Till he unseam'd him from the nave to the chaps,
> And fix'd his head upon our battlements.

If we continue to imagine, think with, and share the feelings of the characters, reading the play will be a most enlightening and enjoyable experience and an excellent preparation for watching an actual performance. As we read about and envision the events before and during the murder of the King by Macbeth, and what follows, we shall appreciate the exquisite language expressing the outstanding qualities of each character. We shall understand Macbeth's gentleness toward his wife, who considers him to be "full o' th' milk of human kindness"; his feelings of guilt and despair as he, the murderer of his King, exclaims, "Will all great Neptune's ocean wash this blood/Clean from my hand?"; and his wife's tigerish courage as she demands, after the murder, "Give me the dagger . . . My hands are of your colour; but I shame/ To wear a heart so white."

Thus we can follow the structure, plots, and human beings throughout the five acts of the play until, in the last, climactic scene on the battlefield, the loyal nobleman,

Macduff, kills Macbeth and brings the murderer's head to Malcolm (son of the murdered King) who graciously invites all the assembled nobles and soldiers to his coronation: "So, thanks to all at once and to each one,/ Whom we invite to see us crown'd at Scone."

A playwright seldom gives us direct information about the events and characters in his play, but lets the settings, conversation, and actions tell us what is most important. Actors, playgoers, and readers must fill in omitted details by using their imagination. One actor will speak the same lines more sharply than another, the interpretations by the audience will vary, and readers, too, will differ in their reactions. Is it not so with events in life also? We cannot expect everyone to think or respond in the same way to any significant problem or situation. As you read, however, you will appreciate and enjoy the play more and more if you attempt to sympathize with the characters and understand why they speak and act as they do.

Reading and Rereading. A first quick reading of a play should provide some familiarity with its main features. Its architectural aspect can be readily understood by noting the various settings, characters, dialogue, climaxes, and conclusion, the highlights which disclose the entire framework. At the same time, the first reading will also reveal changing moods, themes, and plot development—the large blocks of speech and action constituting the colorful, pictorial aspects. The attentive reader will surely enjoy some of the musical aspects, reflected in the outstanding speeches, eloquent expressions, and flow of language. The philosophical aspects, the ideas or messages, may challenge or reinforce his cherished assumptions or stimulate new thoughts. Finally, from the psychological point of view, the reader will react, at least tentatively, to the motives and actions of the principal characters and share their sentiments.

A second reading will deepen and enrich the reader's understanding and interpretation of the play as he views the plot, subplots, dialogue, and events step-by-step, sympathetically acting out the role of each character.

Now he will consider a few points of evaluation: How convincingly are the various problems and situations of the play introduced? What are the most impressive features, such as surprise developments, crises, climaxes, outstanding moods, and memorable remarks? What makes the characters seem real and true to life, or unreal and artificial? As the reader evaluates the play in ways such as these, he will rightly feel himself to be contributing something of his own to it, almost as if he were an actor, a playgoer, or even an assistant to the playwright himself. As he reads aloud, he imagines or impersonates each actor as one who will "suit the action to the word, the word to the action," without overstepping "the modesty of nature" by excessive exaggeration or underemphasis, for the purpose of a play (to quote Shakespeare further) is "to hold as 'twere, the mirror up to nature; to show virtue her own feature, scorn her own image, and the very age and body of the time his form and pressure," making all things real and true to life.

ENJOYMENT OF NOVELS

The novelist usually has much greater opportunity than the poet and dramatist to paint backgrounds or settings, to explore characters and ideas in detail, and to introduce all sorts of illuminating information and comments that will help the reader to understand events, emotions, and human relationships essential to the story. He can describe the personality or motives of characters as if he were able to detect their innermost thoughts. He can devote many pages of description to the locale of the story. He can discuss historical events or social conditions which influence the characters in his novel. He can go back and forth in time and space, make fantastic assumptions about people, institutions, inventions, intermingle realities and truths with dreams and myths. For the sake of the story, readers will accept all such devices insofar as they shed light upon the pattern of events which propel the narrative steadily forward from its beginnings through its climaxes to its end. They expect truth, but not necessarily true details; rather, they look for universal truth about man and nature, truth about what could happen in some kind of world—in the world depicted by the author—be it a world of dreams or a world of reality or both.

Empathy. A novel has at its core a unified story, usually developed by presenting the thoughts, spoken words, and actions of the characters; the plot is supplemented by comments and information which may often tell us much about the backgrounds and traits of the characters. The reader must not only notice what the people in the novel say and do, but he must also interpret the reasons for their behavior, the true reasons or the mere rationalizations, the motives which impel them to act, and the connections between parts of the story. He must imagine himself to be each of the persons being portrayed, putting himself in his place, as if he had the same knowledge and personality and faced the same problem or situation. If there is a single sequence of events as there is in many novels, the reader will find it easy to understand the plot; but if there are numerous disconnected fragments or episodes, or if the story goes backward as well as forward in time, the task of following all the relationships among the parts may become complicated or confusing. In the latter case, the alert reader may reread some of the episodes to refresh his memory so that he can see the entire panorama of the novel as it unfolds—as if it were a unified, growing organism but with some portions growing at different times and more quickly than others.

Like the playreader and playgoer, too, the reader of a novel must evaluate the personality of each character as an individual who speaks to others, and behaves toward them, in the precise manner stated or implied by the story. Often the author will provide direct information about each person's background of experience, attitudes, purposes, and ideas. Such information will help the reader to understand the characters, just as he would after long association with them in real life situations.

The characters may be logical, impulsive, inconsistent, now admirable, later despicable, or even two-faced, and the reader cannot always pigeonhole each person in some narrow moral compartment. As in life, people in a story do not always behave as they normally should. Surprising, inconsistent behavior is a significant fact to be appreciated.

Suspense and Novelty. The plot of a novel is customarily developed from an introductory stage to an intermediate stage of mounting tension which keeps the reader in suspense until a climax is reached. Suspense and novelty are the two most distinctive and enjoyable qualities found in many masterpieces of fiction. There may be numerous suspenseful situations and surprises, lending spice to an appetizing menu. In most novels, the air is cleared at the end, with complexities resolved and the remaining characters either rewarded or punished or passing through new thresholds of experience with this stage of their lives brought to a fitting conclusion.

Consider a novel such as Hawthorne's *Scarlet Letter,* with which many readers will doubtless be familiar. In the introduction, Hawthorne tells us that he based the story upon some old papers and a scarlet cloth, shaped like a letter A, which he had found in the custom-house at Salem, Massachusetts, where in 1846–49 he was employed as a surveyor. Immediately, we are intrigued by this strange symbol "A," and begin to feel suspense.

> My eyes fastened themselves upon the old scarlet letter, and would not be turned aside. Certainly there was some deep meaning in it. . . . I happened to place it on my breast. It seemed to me, then, that I experienced a sensation not altogether physical, yet almost so, as of burning heat; and as if the letter were not of red cloth, but red-hot iron. I shuddered, and involuntarily let it fall upon the floor.

Who could read such passages without becoming most eager, impatient, to read on and on until this mystery of the symbol could be explained?

As we read on, everything bears out the mysterious,

somber atmosphere implied by the author's comment in his introduction. Hawthorne himself explained, in his notes—written, strange as it may seem, in 1844, long before he worked at the custom-house—that he wrote the introduction to "relieve the shadows of the gloomy story." All the characters speak and act in this serious, depressing, tense tone; the story is filled with sadness— tragedy in the events, desperation in its personalities, "unrelieved gloom" even in the descriptions of the locale.

The story begins at a scaffold in the courtyard of a prison in seventeenth-century Puritan Boston, as the convicted adulteress, Hester Prynne, is sentenced to wear the letter "A," the mark of shame, forever on her bosom. The popular minister, Dimmesdale, Hester's lover, calls upon her to name the guilty man (that is, himself), but she refuses. Disputing the justice of man-made laws and penalties, she shields her lover from them and cares devotedly for their daughter, Pearl. Thus we are launched upon a suspenseful adventure, and we cannot pause in our reading but must continue as Hester's aging husband vows revenge upon the unknown guilty man. The somber tone of the novel—the Puritanical obsession with sin, punishment, and death—thus prevails and persists throughout to the end.

Reality and Truth. The reader will note how each main episode is described in the same dramatic terms and tone, reflected alike in the language of the dour, severe characters and the moralistic comments of the author. Thus, when Hester rents a small cottage near the town and works as a seamstress, she defiantly wears her symbol of shame and bears firmly the insults of the Puritan rabble while earning a livelihood with needlework and also sewing "coarse garments" free for the poor. Hawthorne comments: "Lonely as was Hester's situation, and without a friend on earth who dared to show himself, she, however, . . . possessed . . . the art—then, as now, almost the only one within a woman's grasp—of needlework. The child had a native grace . . . So magnificent was the small figure . . . that there was an absolute circle of radiance around her, on the darksome cottage-floor. . . ." Later, in the same mood of sad dignity, the minister, Hester's secret lover, appeals to the authorities to leave the child with Hester: "She recognizes, believe me, the solemn miracle which God hath wrought, in the existence of that child. . . . For Hester Prynne's sake, then, and no less for the poor child's sake, let us leave them as Providence hath seen fit to place them!"

Hawthorne's novel consists of dramatic episodes which fit into the plot as a whole but give the impression of separate events, or separated parts of a chain of events, and the reader must depend upon his own imagination for connecting links between them. We must admire this novelist's fluent language, his ability to develop themes of immense dignity, to create a steady, uniform atmosphere, and to set forth numerous details of speech and action which strongly impress the reader. Perhaps the sustained somber tone of the story reflected Hawthorne's personal experience of tragedy, tension, and poverty in his family, contrasted with the successes of his distinguished ancestors. He felt keenly, as he wrote to Sophia Peabody, "the entangling depths of my obscurity." But he accepted the Puritan concept that sin must be punished. In *The Scarlet Letter* the guilty couple are doomed irrevocably to pay dearly for their sin. Hawthorne understood but condemned the romantic sentiments of his time, the rebellious spirit represented by Hester, yet he also objected to the excessively harsh judgments of society. This attitude may explain why the novel dramatizes the difference between Hester, who sinned on impulse, and her husband, Chillingworth, who deliberately plotted evil and revenge. At the end the author praises Hester for her self-reliance and charity, though he cannot side wholeheartedly with her against the rigid moral standards of Puritanism. Although he pictured Hester as one who believed in her own right to live and love as she chose, Hawthorne attributed her choice to moral weakness, and he attempted to show that "human frailty" would inevitably bring sorrow in its train. Yet, after all, he finally portrayed Hester as a noble woman endowed with patience, courage, and hope for a new morality, a more just and free society.

Thus we see that genuine understanding and enjoyment of a well-written novel require close attention to its pervading principle, to its central truths about human beings, but, more than this, they require of the reader that he identify himself wholeheartedly and sympathetically with the characters, that he make their personal, intimate feelings, problems, moods, and thoughts part of himself, for the characters must through their words and deeds impart reality and truth to the author's work.

8

How To Choose What To Read

The selection of reading materials can be a task so complex and troublesome that some prospective readers may be tempted to give up in despair and take refuge in time-wasting competitive attractions or aimless activities devoid of intellectual, moral, cultural, material, or physical benefits. With more than 250,000 books in print in the United States alone, as well as hundreds of older (out-of-print) books still available to American readers, it is no wonder that many people do not know where to begin the process of selection. How easy it is to turn on the radio or television set and just sit while whatever happens to be presented, good or bad, captures one's attention and too often consumes with trivia a person's most precious asset—the time of his life! On the other hand, the person who prefers to devote his time to worthwhile reading must think for himself, make some intelligent effort, some logical decisions, and some deliberate choices, inquiring into his own needs and interests as he builds a personal library of worthwhile journals and books.

Nevertheless, nothing invested, nothing gained. More and more people, young and old, are reading more—and more intelligently—because they realize that life is short, that it should be lived to the full, that it should be significant, enjoyable, earnest, meaningful, stimulating, creative, educative, and uplifting in the finest sense; and they know that, in modern times, these values can best be achieved through discriminating selection and attentive reading of periodicals, pamphlets, and books, encompassing news, feature articles, poetry, drama, short stories, novels, essays, and works of philosophy, psychology, religion, science, art, music, history, biography, folklore, humor, and other fascinating and useful subjects communicated by means of the printed word.

I do not mean to condemn other media of communication. In fact, there are worthwhile programs on television, including excellent discussions of books, but even the best of its plays, concerts, exhibits, demonstrations, and discussions are often ruined by offensive advertisements for inferior products, prepared by hucksters oblivious to the sensibilities and intellectual sensitivities or interests of the audience. I wonder what would happen if publishers insisted on inserting moronic advertisements for a piece of soap between the stanzas of a great poem, between the scenes of an absorbing drama, or between the paragraphs of a suspenseful novel! Yet commercial television networks utilize the public channels of communication to sell soap and other profitable commodities, not to provide the cultural experiences and wholesome enjoyments for which the airways belonging to the people should be used. How fortunate are those millions of readers who can choose their own entertainment because they have built personal libraries at home and can quickly choose among hundreds or thousands of literary masterpieces and other printed sources of ideas and information, wisely devoting their precious time to them!

SELECTION OF BOOKS

Readers building their personal library of the "best" books will naturally differ in their approach to this formidable task. Some may wish to become familiar with the significant writings in each period of history, beginning perhaps with *The Book of the Dead,* which nearly six thousand years ago set forth ideas (about justice, law, morality, and immortality) still part of our heritage, then reading the literature of each civilization, ancient, medieval, and modern. Other readers may prefer to devote most of their reading time to specific types of literature, in English or in translation, such as poetry, drama, fiction, myths, histories, biographies, essays, or religious, scientific, and philosophical works. Still others may be attracted especially to the writings of some of the most renowned or influential geniuses—a long line of masters of the written word from Vergil to Shakespeare, Goethe, and Shaw, whose works can be read in English and in many other languages. Finally, there are readers who have no set plan or program but simply obtain books through recommendation, reports by critics, displays or advertisements, browsing in stores or libraries, or participation in some class, discussion group, or club.

There is nothing wrong with any of these approaches to the selection of books. Nevertheless, in view of the hundreds of thousands of books available, most readers could benefit from a systematic planning of their selections. I should like, therefore, to suggest a program of book selection which would fit the needs and interests of different types of readers. This program is divided into (1) a core list of books everyone should own and (2) a special list of significant books in literature, philosophy, psychology, religion, science, and the arts. The core list of foundation books will be discussed in the remainder of this chapter. The list of books in special fields will be presented in the next chapter.

A CORE LIST OF BOOKS

The following core list represents an indispensable collection of works of writers and thinkers who have shaped the minds and enriched the lives of all humanity. For this foundation set of books, I have selected the works of thirty authors which have not only been accepted universally as literary masterpieces, or superb examples of a literary form, but have also had an enduring, pervasive influence upon mankind in their own and succeeding ages. The authors, arranged chronologically by date of birth, are: Homer, Aeschylus, Sophocles, Euripides, Aristophanes, Vergil, Plutarch, St. Augustine, Dante, Chaucer, Erasmus, Montaigne, Cervantes, Spenser, Shakespeare, Milton, Molière, Defoe, Swift, Voltaire, Samuel Johnson, Rousseau, Emerson, Dickens, Stowe, Thoreau, Melville, Ibsen, Shaw, and Whitman. Their works include plays, novels, poetry, satire, essays, criticism, and biography. Their writings span a period of 2,800 years, from the birth of Homer ca. 850 B.C. to the death of Shaw in 1950.

Any home which does not possess in its library representative works of all or nearly all of these great authors and thinkers is indeed culturally deprived. There are, of course, hundreds and thousands of other gifted writers whose works and ideas have endured to our time, but surely those named here are indispensable.

Great Dramatists. Our core list contains the names of eight famous playwrights: Aeschylus, Sophocles, Euripides, Aristophanes, Shakespeare, Molière, Ibsen, and Shaw.

AESCHYLUS (525–456 B.C.), author of ninety-two plays, was one of the foremost dramatists of ancient times. He wrote the classical trilogy *Oresteia,* consisting of three interrelated Greek plays depicting the sacrificial murder of his daughter Iphigenia by King Agamemnon to appease the goddess Artemis, a deed which causes so much pain to his wife Clytemnestra the Queen (the "pain that never sleeps") that in revenge, with the aid of her lover, she murders the victorious King on his return from the conquest of Troy; the murder of the Queen and her lover by her own son Orestes and daughter Electra to avenge their father follows; and, finally, divine forgiveness is granted the conscience-stricken son for his crime of matricide. The drama teaches that horrible, unnatural sins must be punished, but that there is hope of forgiveness for the criminal who has acted from a sense of duty and has suffered torment of conscience and sought atonement for his sin.

(There are various editions and translations of the trilogy, including *Oresteia,* translated by Richmond Lattimore, edited by David Grene and Richmond Lattimore, paperbound, published by the University of Chicago Press; also, 3 volumes, paperbound, translated by Gilbert Murray, published by Oxford University Press. Be sure to read, too, another classical drama by Aeschylus: *Prometheus Bound,* translated by Gilbert Murray, paperbound, published by Oxford University Press.)

SOPHOCLES (ca. 496–406 B.C.), Athenian genius, wrote the masterpieces *Oedipus the King* (or *Oedipus Tyrannus*), *Oedipus at Colonus, Antigone,* and other superbly constructed dramas. The background of *Oedipus the King* is that the King and Queen of Thebes are warned by an oracle that their son Oedipus, soon to be born, will murder the King and have incestuous relations with his mother, the Queen, so they order the newborn infant to be tied up and exposed to die. Their order is not obeyed, and Oedipus grows up to carry out the predicted crimes, though without knowing the identities of his victims. In the play, a plague strikes the city and, it is believed, will not pass until the old King's murderer is punished. When the truth is revealed, the Queen hangs herself and Oedipus inflicts upon himself the terrible punishment (blinding) which he had decreed for the then unknown murderer.

(Read *Sophocles I, Three Tragedies,* and *Sophocles II, Four Tragedies,* two paperbound volumes edited by David Grene and Richmond Lattimore, published by the University of Chicago Press.)

EURIPIDES (ca. 480–402 B.C.) was a revolutionary Greek dramatist, realistic, and more modern than many modern playwrights. In his plays he explored the psychological conflicts within the soul of man as he struggles heroically against human and natural evils, against war, cruelty, and injustice, and against man's inhumanity to man—burdens from which he must free himself without help from the gods or fickle fortune. Euripides' *Medea* is one of the most moving, vivid, and "modern" plays ever written, a play about Jason (of Golden Fleece fame), a royal mismarriage, an unfaithful husband, and the terrible revenge taken by his jealous, betrayed wife. *The Trojan Women* is the most eloquent peace propaganda ever written, depicting the pitiful fate of the women of Troy carried off as slaves by the Greek conquerors of their native land: "piteously . . . weeping, with fear striking our hearts, for we are slaves."

(Read *Medea, The Trojan Women,* and eight other plays in *Ten Plays by Euripides,* a compact paperbound volume of translations by Moses Hadas and John Harvey McLean, published by Bantam Books.)

ARISTOPHANES (ca. 448–380 B.C.), Greek master of plays containing beautifully musical poetry and powerful propaganda, bitterly opposed Euripides' ideal of individual self-direction and wrote hilarious comedies (such as *The Frogs* and *The Clouds*) which ridiculed the literary, political, and intellectual leaders of Athens, exposed and condemned the corruption, mobocracy, immorality, and hypocrisy of his time, attacked the new ideas of Socrates (who wanted everyone to think for himself about truth, beauty, and morality), and pleaded, as some conservative writers might today, for a return to old traditions and simple ideals in government, literature, and education. Of eleven comedies extant (out of more than forty he wrote), *Lysistrata* is a most wonderful, fun-filled farce of special interest to modern readers because it tells how the women of Athens and Sparta used every conceivable means of stopping the senseless war between the two nations and even refused to live with their husbands unless the men made peace. Their strategy was successful in restoring tranquility and harmony.

(Read *Lysistrata, The Frogs, The Clouds,* and two other plays by Aristophanes in the paperbound volume, *Five Comedies of Aristophanes,* translated by Benjamin B. Rogers, edited by Andrew Chiappe, published by Doubleday & Co., Inc.)

SHAKESPEARE, WILLIAM (1564–1616) was the greatest of dramatists and the greatest of poets; his art continues to remake the minds of men, inspiring them through its architectural perfection, masterly portrayal of human nature and universal truths, depth of meaning, exquisite eloquence, and wisdom. Of Shakespeare the man we know so little that controversies rage about his identity. The best answer to the question, "Who was Shakespeare?" is a quotation from one of his own works: "That which we call a rose by any other name would smell as sweet." His colleague, Ben Jonson, tells us, in a brief but significant appraisal of Shakespeare's character, that "he was indeed honest and of an open and free nature." That comment helps to explain why everything this greatest of all masters wrote was more nearly real and true to life and nature, and more nearly perfect, than the works of any other writer before or since. There has been but one Shakespeare, however he be named, and mankind may rightly boast of genuine cultural progress in some future age if another such as he is born.

I recommended a few years ago that leading Shakespearean scholars be invited to prepare a series of explanatory guidebooks to accompany the bard's original works, and the distinguished editor selected for the task of editing the series completed a national survey to determine which of Shakespeare's thirty-seven plays are being most widely read. The most popular plays were found to be the six tragedies of *Macbeth, Julius Caesar, Hamlet, Romeo and Juliet, Othello,* and *King Lear,* and two comedies, *The Merchant of Venice* and *A Midsummer Night's Dream.* (The number of young readers in their teens ranged from 130,000 for *A Midsummer Night's Dream* to 1,260,000 for *Macbeth.*)

All these magnificent plays are available in numerous low-priced paperbound editions, as well as in handsome hardbound editions, and all should become treasured volumes in every home. In addition, there are several excellent paperbound editions of Shakespeare's *Sonnets,* the most nearly perfect poetry ever written. Bookstores and libraries stock attractive one-volume editions of Shakespeare's complete works in a durable cloth binding, as well as numerous special collections of plays—volumes of four plays, of five plays, of eight plays, of comedies, of tragedies, and of histories, many in paperbound editions.

In *Hamlet,* the most famous and influential of all plays, Hamlet is the enigmatic, hesitant, melancholy, tragic prince of Denmark who, despite his native sensitivity and romantic idealism, faces a terrible moral dilemma and inner conflict as he is impelled to revenge the murder of the King, his father, by the "incestuous, murderous, damned Dane," the murdered King's brother. Yet Hamlet must make certain, first, that his uncle actually committed the murder, and second, that if his uncle should prove to be guilty, Hamlet can bring him to justice and at the same time win public approval for ridding the nation of a fratricidal villain. By mistake, Hamlet impulsively kills the King's Lord Chamberlain, Polonius, a "wretched, rash, intruding fool," instead of the guilty King. Hamlet's sweetheart, Ophelia, daughter of Polonius, is driven mad by the Prince's weird behavior and commits suicide. The furious plots and counterplots of the two main antagonists—Hamlet and his uncle, the usurper —end in the final duel scene of the last act with the violent deaths of the three royal characters: the Queen, the King, and Hamlet himself. (This play is available in sixteen paperbound editions.)

Macbeth, too, is a powerful tragedy centering in regicide and the usurpation of a throne, that of Scotland. As in *Hamlet,* so in *Macbeth* an overambitious pair contrives to assassinate their King. Here the royal victim is Duncan, "gracious ruler," whose generosity and "virtues will plead like angels against the deep damnation of his taking-off; . . ." As in *Hamlet,* the plot in *Macbeth* ends with the violent deaths of the usurper and his accomplice. I include excerpts from *Macbeth* on page 137. (There are seventeen paperbound editions of this play available.)

Julius Caesar depicts the assassination of the greatest military genius, "mighty Caesar," who ruled the Roman world "like a Colossus," but whose vanity and ambition brought about his downfall. His traitorous friend Brutus, patriotic, gullible leader of the assassins, called him "the noblest Roman of them all." The play traces the fate of the assassins from the aftermath of the conspiracy and murder to the final battle scene where both of their commanders (Brutus and the shrewd, cynical Cassius with the "lean and hungry look") are defeated by the loyal Mark Anthony, "well beloved" friend of Caesar, and Octavius, Caesar's grandnephew and heir, and commit suicide. This greatest of political plays is lifelike and powerful in every scene and action as it relates the events which decided not only the fates of individual characters but also the destiny of the Roman republic and turned into a new direction the entire course of world history. (There are thirteen paperbound editions of *Julius Caesar* in print.)

In *Romeo and Juliet*, Romeo, heir of the wealthy Montague family of Verona, who is at first an infatuated sensualist, is transformed by his trysts with Juliet (whose beauty "doth teach the torches to burn bright") into "gentle Romeo," a sincere, honorable, sensitive, impetuous lover. Juliet, a girl of fourteen, daughter of the Capulet family (bitter enemies of the Montagues) fears that disaster impends but dreams of her true love, defies parents and convention, breaking a promise to accept her mother's choice of a husband for her, and seizes the happiness of devoted, mutual love with Romeo which, however, she insists must be genuine, reciprocal, and thoroughly honest on both sides:

> "O swear not by the moon, the inconstant moon . . .
> Lest that thy love prove likewise variable."

The feud between the lovers' families divides the entire city into warring factions and sharpens the significance of the young couple's secret marriage in defiance of parental authority. Their elopement, however, is doomed by tragic accidents and mistakes of judgment, ending in the suicide of both unhappy lovers. Only then are the two families reconciled, too late to prevent tragedy, yet at last uniting the divided city. (Twelve paperbound editions of *Romeo and Juliet* are available.)

Othello, the Moor of Venice, tells the story of Othello, the proud Moorish nobleman and general who, being "great of heart" and "of a free and open nature," believes that only his accounts of dangerous exploits had won for him the love and loyalty of the gracious beauty Desdemona, daughter of the Venetian nobleman and senator, Brabantio. Their elopement (compare it with the similar elopement of Romeo and Juliet) met with the bitter opposition of her father, who turned against them, especially since he had favored a more attractive suitor for his daughter's hand. Othello is driven insanely jealous by the hints of his villainous ensign, Iago, that Desdemona has betrayed him for the sake of a handsome lieutenant, Cassio. Enraged by Iago's planted evidence (including Cassio's possession of a handkerchief—Othello's first gift to Desdemona), the Moor strangles his wife in bed as she desperately pleads innocence; then, learning the truth about the trusted villain's perfidy, he kills Iago, stabs himself, and kissing the lifeless lips of his innocent Desdemona, exclaims in his dying moments:

> "I kiss'd thee ere I kill'd thee . . . no way but this,
> Killing myself, to die upon a kiss."

(Ten paperbound editions of *Othello* are available.)

King Lear is a doubly tragic story about two old men and their children, whose characters they misjudge with disastrous consequences. King Lear is the headstrong, foolhardy, stern, and proud ruler of Britain who demands of his three daughters that they proclaim their complete devotion and loyalty to him above and beyond any other obligations, proving themselves worthy of being heirs to his kingdom. Two deceitful daughters ("gilded serpents," "tigers, not daughters") make a pretense of their love for him, but the third and youngest, his favorite Cordelia (whose voice "was ever soft, gentle, and low"), tells him the truth—that she cares for him as a daughter should, yet reserves her deepest affection for some future husband. In a sudden, topsy-turvy misunderstanding of his daughters' real motives, Lear disowns the honest, loyal

Cordelia and hands over his realm to the two cruel, greedy daughters who later mistreat him horribly and cast him out to madness in the countryside. Similarly, the second rash, gullible, old man, the Earl of Gloucester, a faithful supporter of Lear's, makes a crucial mistake about his own two sons, punishing the loyal, legitimate son, Edgar, and rewarding the evil, traitorous, "rough and lecherous" bastard son, Edmund. Gloucester is tortured and blinded by Lear's wicked daughter Regan and her husband, but the latter and the two evil daughters, the "she-foxes," meet a violent death, one daughter poisoning the other and then stabbing herself to death. Meanwhile, Gloucester's bastard son Edmund, then commander of the British army, has seized Lear and hanged the gentle Cordelia. In the last scene of the play, the pitiful Lear dies with her dead body in his arms. (There are ten paperbound editions of *King Lear* available.)

In the *Merchant of Venice,* the merchant is the generous, loyal Antonio who pledges his own body as security when his friend Bassanio borrows from the vengeful moneylender, Shylock (a Jew who hates the Christians for their insults and is enraged further when his daughter steals his money and elopes with a Christian), money needed for his expenses in paying court to the beautiful, virtuous, gracious Portia, fair lady whose "sunny locks" hang upon "her temples like a golden fleece." Bassanio wins the fair lady by choosing the correct casket while blindfolded in a contest against other suitors. When misfortune prevents Antonio from repaying the loan, Shylock demands his "pound of flesh," rejecting Portia's plea for mercy:

> "The quality of mercy is not strain'd,
> It droppeth as the gentle rain from heaven
> upon the place beneath. . . ."

Portia, disguised as a noted lawyer, has been invited to serve as judge in the case. She renders judgment strictly —ruling that, in accordance with the contract for the loan, the moneylender must not shed a drop of blood nor take even an ounce more or less than one pound of Antonio's flesh, thus circumventing the terms of the contract—and then imposes on Shylock a severe penalty for illegally plotting against the life of Antonio, a Venetian citizen. The play ends with justice done, friendship and love rewarded, as Portia discloses her disguise to Bassanio. (This play is available in fifteen paperbound editions.)

A Midsummer Night's Dream is a delightful comedy reflecting the two themes that "the course of true love never did run smooth" and that the enchantment of moon-struck lovers, whether produced by their "seething brains" "that apprehend more than cool reason ever comprehends" or by love potions prepared by fairies, impels them to act like madmen, for "the lunatic, the lover and the poet" are alike, and "Lord, what fools these mortals be!" This play is a magical, fantastic one with a happy ending for three pairs of lovers—after merry entanglements and woodland adventures—as the fairies bless "with sweet peace" the sleeping lovers in their chambers and also their future children so that they will be born perfect with never a "mole, harelip, nor scar, nor mark prodigious, such as are despised in nativity. . . ." (There are nine paperbound editions of this play available.)

MOLIÈRE, JEAN BAPTISTE POQUELIN (1622–1673) was the greatest of French playwrights and comparable to Shakespeare in the creation of lifelike comedies exposing people as they are in themselves—weak, selfish, capricious, cunning, deceitful—not sincere, charitable, wise, and pious, as they appear to be on the surface. Each comedy strikes at a central weakness of human nature, and many of the comedies reveal the truth about unscrupulous scoundrels and their gullible victims.

Molière's *Tartuffe* was at first the most hated of comedies because church leaders interpreted the play as an attack upon them. One called Molière a "demon clad in human flesh" and suggested that burning him in eternal fires of hell would not be too harsh a punishment. Actually, the play (which Molière rewrote again and again) condemned religious impostors, not religion. Tartuffe, the

pious hypocrite, poses as a grateful, self-sacrificing fol-
lower of the church, induces the wealthy Orgon to hand
over all his property to him, encourages plans for marriage with Orgon's daughter, and then is caught making
love to Orgon's wife. All ends well for everybody except
the scoundrel Tartuffe.

In *Don Juan*, Molière pays his respects to those unscrupulous aristocratic libertines who excuse their vices
on the specious ground that "everybody is doing it," when,
of course, it is mostly they themselves who are "doing it."
The plot is based on Tirso de Molina's play about the
Spanish legend of Don Juan (in which the villain betrays
Don Gonzalo's daughter, kills the father in a duel, and is
strangled by a statue of Gonzalo). In Molière's version,
Don Juan abducts and marries a convent girl, then deserts
her, rationalizing that it had been a sin anyway to have
taken her from God's service for sake of marriage to a
man like him, a free-and-easy lover of all women. He
cunningly promises to repent and reform but knows he
never will, for he has no real faith in heaven or hell but
only in his own pleasures.

Other comedies portray similar human frailties, greed,
and deceit. *The Miser* is about rich Harpagon, who cares
for nothing but money and uses his son and daughter to
get more of it. But all his schemes are in the end frus-
trated. *The Misanthrope* is based on the theme that stupid,
stubborn people must expect disaster such as afflicted the
hero Alceste, unhappy lover of the fickle flirt Célimène.
The Doctor in Spite of Himself tells about a medical im-
postor whose deceits fool most people but eventually
boomerang; however, the faker is saved from hanging,
and all turns out well.

(Read *The Misanthrope and Other Plays,* five plays
translated by John Wood, including *Tartuffe* and *The
Doctor in Spite of Himself*; and *The Miser and Other
Plays,* five plays translated by John Wood, including *Don
Juan.*)

IBSEN, HENRIK (1828–1906), creative gift of Norway
to the literature, the culture, and the social progress of

Europe and Western civilization, found himself ostracized in his native land because his plays attacked established institutions and illuminated the sore thumbs of society. His plays call a spade a spade, telling the facts of life about the game of life and all the players in it. He had no final answers to social problems but exposed the double standard—the gap between what people want others to do and what they themselves do, between high ideals and evil practices, between the rare, honest, unself-ish person and the multitudes of cowards, hypocrites, and stubborn self-seekers who fear and resist reforms which might upset their genuine ambitions.

A Doll's House exposes the false morality which kept unhappy wives tied by convention to their husbands who used them to bolster their own pride, treated them like innocent dolls and often like slaves, and thus deprived them of their identities as human beings, their minds and souls as individuals. The condition of women has im-proved in Western countries since Ibsen's time—read Ashley M. F. Montagu's *The Natural Superiority of Women*, reflecting a new attitude of respect for the female sex. In Ibsen's view, the abuse of women by their male masters was only one aspect of the despicable social order, with its injustice, cruelty, disillusionment, and obstinate blindness to the truth. The wife, Nora, changes from a traditional doll-like, contriving, submissive crea-ture into a passionate rebel against unjust laws and customs, a rebel who abandons husband and children in order to become a whole human being in her own right, an individual.

Other representative plays by this master dramatist are *Brand*, in which an honest preacher is utterly de-stroyed by his congregation when he expects them to prac-tice the religious ideas to which they give lip service; *The Pillars of Society*, which shows how the most respected leaders of the community conceal skeletons in dark closets—in this drama truth is discovered and genuine repentance follows; *Ghosts*, which depicts the immoral blindness of church and society to scientific facts, such as the spread of venereal disease; *An Enemy of the People*, which shows what happens when the so-called "good people" of a community face the challenge of someone who insists on telling the truth about their germ-polluted water supply (how modern this story about pollution seems today!); *Hedda Gabler,* which portrays an evil, domineering woman who brings pain and destruction to everyone, including herself; and *The Master Builder,* which tells how the fondest, hidden dreams of gifted creative persons may remain buried in the depths of their inner being, resulting in a lack of perfect fulfillment which can drive them on and on to desperation and catastrophe.

(Read *Six Plays,* a book in the Modern Library with an introduction by Eva Le Gallienne and including *A Doll's House, Ghosts, An Enemy of the People, Rosmersholm, Hedda Gabler,* and *The Master Builder; Brand,* translated by Michael Meyer; *Peer Gynt,* translated by Michael Meyer; and *The Wild Duck,* translated and edited by Kai Jurgenson and Robert F. Schenkkan.)

SHAW, GEORGE BERNARD (1856–1950), who admired and defended Ibsen as "a man of genius," wrote with the same sympathy for the oppressed and unfortunate (for example, the patient neglected by doctors who treat people as things, not as people), condemning cruelty of all kinds, including the torture of animals for profit (he was a vegetarian because he respected and valued all living creatures). No one knew better than Shaw what he intended to do in his plays, and no one expressed his intentions more pointedly and convincingly than he did in the prefaces to his first two books of plays (*Plays: Pleasant and Unpleasant*) published in 1898, in which he wrote in behalf of the "general onslaught on idealism . . . implicit in *Arms and the Man* and the realistic plays of the modern school." He was no longer "satisfied with fictitious morals and fictitious good conduct, shedding fictitious glory on overcrowding, disease, crime, drink, war, cruelty, infant mortality, and all the other commonplaces of civilization which drive men to the theatre to make foolish pretenses that these things are progress, science, morals, religion, patriotism, imperial supremacy, national greatness and all other names the newspapers call them." We find this attitude of respect for truth and reality in Shaw's great predecessors Shakespeare, Molière, and Ibsen, but Shaw wrote in a sophisticated, brilliant style about paradoxical situations and ideas which delighted his audiences of well-to-do theatergoers, each of whom felt clearsighted enough to appreciate the facts of life as revealed in the plays in contrast with the foolish dreams and misconceptions afflicting "less clearsighted people."

Shaw fought for Ibsen because he shared the latter's devotion to the cause of individual freedom and social reform. There is no question about Shaw's sincerity, reflected in his influential leadership of the Fabian Socialists in England as well as in his exposure of social hypocrisy and inhumanity by means of his masterly plays. In addition to the plays, be sure to read Shaw's essays, "The Economic Basis of Socialism" and "The Transition to Social Democracy," in *Fabian Essays in Socialism,* and other essays in the paperbound volume, *Selected Non-Dramatic Writings of George Bernard Shaw,* edited by Dan H. Laurence. Read also *Shaw on Music,* brilliant selections compiled by Eric Bentley, now available in paperbound format.

Among the early Shaw plays were *The Widower's Houses* and *Mrs. Warren's Profession,* both contrasting the standards people profess to believe in with the things they actually believe and do.

The Widower's Houses has as its central theme the commonplace truth that young men with high theoretical ideals are easily corrupted by evil institutions, the establishment, of their community. Dr. Trench refuses to marry the daughter of a slum landlord because she will bring him tainted money which he discovers to have been earned through illegal neglect of houses for poor tenants. But then he is shocked to learn that his own small income has for years been derived from illegal and immoral profits from the same properties, on which he held mortgages. When his accustomed income is endangered, he decides to live with the evils he had always condemned as shameful—a familiar story today as we see young people meekly take their comfortable places as obedient robots in the worst of our contemporary enterprises. Shaw would admire the young men and women who dare to defy immoral institutions and customs.

Mrs. Warren's profession of prostitution, in *Mrs. Warren's Profession*, complicates her sheltered daughter's romance with a young man who turns out to be the son of one of her former lovers (a clergyman) and therefore her daughter's half-brother. Mrs. Warren's business partner and financier, the aristocrat Sir George Crofts, offers marriage to her daughter Vivie, but Vivie is horrified to learn from him the true source of her income (compare this with the similar discovery by Dr. Trench in *The Widower's Houses*). At the end, Vivie says good-bye forever to her half-brother and to her mother, resolved to earn her own living in a decent way: "If I had been you, Mother," she says, "I might have done as you did; but I should not have lived one life and believed in another. You are a conventional woman at heart. That is why I am bidding you good-bye now."

Important plays by Shaw include *Arms and the Man*, which ridicules silly notions of military glory; *Candida*, which contrasts poetic love and practical common sense; *Man and Superman*, in which the revolutionary philosopher John Tanner, a disciple of Nietzsche, succumbs to the life force of a superwoman, Ann; *The Man of Destiny*, about Napoleon, who admits there is "only one universal passion: fear . . . It is fear that makes men fight . . . Pooh! there's no such thing as a real hero"; *Major Barbara*, about Barbara, major in the Salvation Army and daughter of a munitions maker whose cause wins out in the end when the daughter and her lover, a professor of Greek, rejoin the world of practicality and realism; *Saint Joan*, about a clever, humane, brave Joan of Arc, who is eventually vindicated and canonized; *Pyg-*

malion, ironic portrayal of high society which anyone willing to work hard enough can be trained by linguistic experts to fit into quite comfortably. Read also *Back to Methuselah, Caesar and Cleopatra, Heartbreak House, The Devil's Disciple, The Doctor's Dilemma*—all of them important plays now available in paperbound editions.)

Great Novelists. There are hundreds, even thousands, of famous novelists whose works deserve an honored place in the home library. For the indispensable list of core books, I have chosen the following five novelists whose writings are loved and admired throughout the Western world: Cervantes, Defoe, Dickens, Stowe, and Melville.

CERVANTES SAAVEDRA, MIGUEL DE (1547–1616), a contemporary of Shakespeare, write numerous stories, poems, and plays, yet none but the novel *Don Quixote* could be called a masterpiece, and none brought him more than the barest sustenance. He died in the same year as Shakespeare, a poor man, renowned, however, for his one great work which had a profound influence upon the society of his time and stimulated the minds of men in succeeding ages up to the present. *Don Quixote* (begun while the author was in prison for debt) portrays hundreds of characters, from the poorest to the richest, as they go about their selfish, illogical business of everyday living in the midst of illusion and self-deception, yet ready to beat down the idealistic dreamer and reformer, who is compelled at last to acknowledge that the world is a world of rogues and schemers who have no use for the chivalrous knights and virtuous ladies idealized in the literature of that materialistic age. Cervantes might have asked himself what would happen if someone really believed the fantastic stories about noble knights and fair ladies and went forth into the world with his head full of such dreams. *Don Quixote* was the answer, for Don Quixote soon discovers how quickly the foolish hypocrites and schemers will resent and resist the right-minded reformers, the simpleminded dreamers like Don Quixote, who mistake what is for what should be, fight windmills they mistake for giants, and eventually die in despair.

(There are several excellent translations of *Don Quixote* available in paperbound editions, including an unabridged edition translated by Walter Starkie. There is also a paperbound volume, *The Portable Cervantes*, containing most of *Don Quixote* and two of his short novels, translated and edited by Samuel Putnam.)

DEFOE, DANIEL (1659?–1731) was about sixty years old when he turned to the writing of fiction after a checkered career as a journalist and secret government agent. He wrote *Robinson Crusoe*, a fascinating story in autobiographical form about a self-reliant British hero, based on the real experiences of a sailor who had lived five years on a deserted island; *Moll Flanders*, about a frail, passionate woman of loose morals (Twelve Years a Whore, Twelve Years a Thief, and so on) but later reformed and retired in wealth; *A Journal of the Plague Year*, an extraordinarily vivid description of what might have been and probably were the horrible events of the great plague of 1665 in London; *Roxana, the Fortunate Mistress*, a story about a greedy, repulsive sex-pot who ended her mad career in tragic wretchedness; and numerous minor works reflecting his personal dogmatic religion-based morality, painstaking attention to details and logic, but utter lack of any appreciation of love and sentiment, for he painted everything either black or white, and nothing in between could be tolerated.

Robinson Crusoe is Defoe's universally admired masterpiece, ingenious, and highly convincing because of the author's meticulous attention to the tiniest details affecting the shipwrecked sailor's struggle to survive alone, as he did for twenty-five years, on the deserted island. The story reads like a detective thriller, each problem being handled with perfect logic and practicality, whether it be building a shelter, making a chair, planting corn, or trapping wild goats—a perfect tribute to the ability of an independent, resourceful Englishman, stripped bare of most of the resources of civilization, but able to overcome nature and win the battle for survival with his two hands and the consoling help of the Good Book, his constant guide and companion.

(Read, in addition to *Robinson Crusoe*—available now in a half-dozen paperbound editions as well as in attractive hardbounds—*Captain Singleton* [about adventures in Africa], *Moll Flanders*, *A Journal of the Plague Year*, and *Roxana, the Fortunate Mistress*.)

DICKENS, CHARLES (1812–1870) was one of the most gifted and prolific creators of literary masterpieces in modern times. He was a genius of very little schooling who worked as a child in a blacking factory and later as a reporter, turning to his true occupation as a novelist at twenty-four years of age. His first two novels were *The Pickwick Papers* (published initially in serial form), in which he touched the spirits of all readers by infusing the story with lively, happy characters and incidents, and *Oliver Twist*, in which he touched the hearts of all readers by portraying the tragic, sorrowful, cruel, and bitter sides of places and persons.

In *The Pickwick Papers*, Mr. Pickwick is misunderstood by his landlady, Mrs. Bardell, who mistakes his remarks for a proposal of marriage and then sues him for breach of promise. He is convicted and ordered to pay damages but prefers to go to the horrible, grim debtors' prison instead. Mrs. Bardell, too, is sent to prison because she cannot pay the costs of the case. Everything is straightened out when Mr. Pickwick pays the costs for her, she withdraws her complaint, and both are released from prison. Many exciting, humorous incidents fill the pages of *The Pickwick Papers*, a most enjoyable example of Dickens's imaginative and inimitable style.

In *Oliver Twist*, Oliver is born in a poorhouse (shortly before his mother dies) and lives nine years in the almshouse, from which he is expelled to work as an apprentice for an undertaker. He falls into the hands of the master teacher of pickpockets, Fagin, who takes him along to watch his pickpockets pick pockets. Being innocent, Oliver stands his ground, is captured by the police and taken to court, but is befriended by the pickpockets' intended victim, Mr. Branlow. He is then kidnapped by Nancy, a girl in Fagin's gang, and forced to watch a burglary. Nancy, who has discovered Oliver's true identity as the heir to a fortune, discloses the truth even though she is then beaten to death by her lover, Sikes of the Fagin gang. The facts of poverty, crime, deceit, and the tribulations of well-meaning people are vividly portrayed so that they become real to us, just as real as the same deplorable facts in our own society today.

In *David Copperfield,* another sad story about poverty and despair, one of the world's prime masterpieces, based in part on Dickens' own life, David's father dies when David is only six months old, and his mother marries again, this time a cruel, tyrannous man who sends David off to a harsh life in school. Later David makes his honest way in the world, experiencing various crises familiar in the lives of the poor, losing loved ones and best friends, but, always with a kindly thought for others, finally settling down with a loving wife, Agnes Wickford, who has ever been his sympathetic inspiration.

A Tale of Two Cities is a stirring novel about the French Revolution and the Reign of Terror, a story filled with emotion, bravery, passion, self-sacrifice, violence— characters like the cold, bloodthirsty Madame Defarge, knitting while she counts the number of heads being chopped off by the guillotine, and Sidney Carton, the English lawyer who calmly gives his life to save the life of the man loved by the woman he himself loves. This superb masterwork captures the hearts and minds of all its readers, young and old, and sustains attention from its first page to the last through unforgettable, dramatic events and personalities.

(Read also *Great Expectations,* about Pip, the boy who, when his expectation of an inheritance is disappointed, becomes a blacksmith but learns to distinguish the real and the good from the false and the evil in life; *Hard Times,* about hard times in a dirty, sooty town dominated by the villainous rich man, Bounderby, and about his unfortunate mill workers who dared to expect education for their children but were themselves misled by a greedy demagogue; the famous story, *A Christmas Carol,* about the transformation of an old miser into a kindly man of charity; *Bleak House, Dombey and Son,* and *Our Mutual Friend,* all exposés of the slum conditions of London in Dickens' time, conditions quite familiar to us in our own land today. Read these masterpieces available in numerous paperbound editions as well as hardbound editions.)

STOWE, HARRIET ELIZABETH BEECHER (1811–1896) wrote several fine works *(The Minister's Wooing, Sam Lawson's Old Town, Old Town Folks, The Pearl of Orr's Island, Palmetto Leaves)* but of course her imperishable work of social literature was *Uncle Tom's Cabin,* now available in numerous paperbound and clothbound editions.

Uncle Tom's Cabin, Lincoln is reported to have said, was written by the little lady who caused the tragic Civil War, but he was mistaken. The Civil War was caused, not by this masterpiece of social literature which aroused the sympathy of decent people in the North and abroad, but mainly by the clash of crass materialistic interests of North and South. Mrs. Stowe's book became a propaganda weapon in the battle between economic rivals, and it failed to remedy the disease of racism which eventually spread throughout the land. The black people in her novel were rightly portrayed as patiently suffering, brave, idealistic, and far superior in many ways to the southern aristocracy whose inhumanity brought the nation to the brink of ruin. The proofs of universal racism accumulated during the century after the end of that war until at last the fact became undeniable that the majority of whites and their leaders, North and South alike, have always been unjust, cruel, and stupid in their human relationships.

It is with special satisfaction that I point to my own writing in the volume *Education and Society* in which, several decades before a Presidential commission (The

Kerner Commission of the Johnson regime) arrived at the same conclusion, I deplored the rank mistreatment of American minorities in their own country and demanded an end to that injustice and a beginning of the effort to make amends for the past. My message was read by a few thousand teachers of whom perhaps a half-dozen paid serious attention. Americans have needed more than one *Uncle Tom's Cabin* in a century to remind them of their passivity in the face of injustice; they need to read great books of this kind every year in every decade if they are to achieve a sane and just society. The majority and their leaders are rightly concerned today, but chiefly for the wrong reason—namely for the reason that violence, riots, and even the danger of revolution are at last threatening their peace of mind and comfort, as the desperate black, Spanish, Mexican, and Indian minorities, comprising thirty million people (whose cause is supported by millions of decent persons in the majority), are ready to fight and die for their basic human rights. In another civil war or guerrilla war, the property and lives of many people would be destroyed. Instead of violence and another civil war, then, let us read *Uncle Tom's Cabin*.

Uncle Tom's Cabin told a little of the truth about that huge concentration camp, the entire region of the South, in 1852, but where are the great novelists who have told the truth about the concentration camp of the entire society, imprisoning the souls of minorities, North and South, East and West, throughout the intervening century? So I write another warning: Be sure to read again *Uncle Tom's Cabin* and be sure that every child reads it again and again, if you wish to see a lasting, decent social order in the nation. I repeat my message of the year 1942: "Is it not hypocritical to preach democracy while denying any minority the chance to live free, useful, happy lives? . . . Our best facilities and educational opportunities ought to be given to the victims of discrimination, to our oppressed minorities." Do read *Uncle Tom's Cabin* again and ask yourself, *Am I my brother's keeper?* The days of noble, patient, kindly, suffering Uncle Toms are gone forever, and this nation must choose either to divide itself again in hatred, bloodshed, and inevitable ruin, or unite justice with brotherhood and mutual respect.

MELVILLE, HERMAN (1819–1891), although locally known for his published stories, was otherwise an unrecognized, unacknowledged genius during his lifetime, who worked as a ship's cabin boy, whaler, farmer, and sailor in the United States Navy. In 1851 he wrote America's great epic, *Moby Dick,* which is now appreciated as an enduring masterpiece of world literature.

Moby Dick is the huge, whiteheaded whale whose sharp, snapping jaws had cut off Captain Ahab's leg like a flash of lightning when the captain attempted to kill him to get tons of precious oil and his teeth and jawbone. Ahab's pious mind and ungodly heart are filled with hate as he vows to find Moby Dick and take revenge. Only Starbuck, the first mate, and Ishmael the sailor (Melville) who lived to tell the tale, understand that the whale had, like all God's creatures, done nothing but defend itself, that man is a mad and evil brute when he seeks vengeance on a dumb animal which is driven to attack his attackers in order to survive in a hostile universe. But Captain Ahab hates the whale for its power and strength; he must have vengeance against even the sun if it should seem to insult him. To him Moby Dick is the symbol of all the insuperable obstacles which evil men face and fear during their short and tragic careers. More sensible is the British captain Boomer, whose arm was snapped off by Moby Dick's teeth, for he feels no malice and keeps out of the monster's way. Other boats and crews are lost in the mad chase to harpoon the whale until at last Ahab in his boat sights him—but Moby Dick rises under the boat and snaps it in two; sighted again next morning, Moby Dick entangles himself and a mauled sailor in the ropes, smashes two more boats to pieces, and hurls Ahab and his boat high into the air.

The next day, the whale is attacked again, and now he

smashes the ship itself. Ahab's harpoon strikes hard, yet only infuriates the whale, whose mad rush forward fouls the rope and thus hurls Ahab to his death. Ishmael, clinging to a canoe, is picked up by a passing ship— Ishmael the wanderer, sole survivor of a man's mad defiance of nature, sole survivor of the wicked attempt of evil-hearted vengeful man to hunt and kill and prove himself to be the evil thing he knows himself to be, a creature who follows vengeance and hate instead of God and love.

(Read this intensely passionate adventure tale of man in a brief, wild encounter with nature—read it in any of thirteen excellent paperbound editions or in an attractive clothbound edition published for your permanent home library.)

Melville's captain in *Billy Budd* is the perfect model of stupid, stubborn (do not these qualities go together?), hidebound, rigid military officers throughout history, oblivious to the true distinction between the spirit and the letter of the law—destroying in their vicious self-pride the minds and hearts of men while pretending to defend the people—the perfect model of the most arrogant, deceitful gang of cowards convinced of their duty and posing as heroic leaders of their gullible fellows. Only on their own deathbeds, if then and when it is too late, can they, like the captain in *Billy Budd*, catch a fleeting glimpse of the truth about life and death, the true consequences of what they have done against the souls of men and nations.

Innocent Billy Budd, impressed into the British Navy, is falsely accused of conspiring to mutiny, and he strikes out at his accuser, the mad ship's officer Claggart. When Claggart dies, Billy is sentenced to death by Captain Vere, who could love Billy almost as a son but is obsessively devoted to strict discipline and the law which prescribes the death penalty for killing an officer. Later the captain is himself killed in battle, dying griefstricken, knowing as a God-fearing man that he has killed an innocent human being, but still convinced that he has done his military duty, though now it is too late for him to be rewarded on earth as a good captain should. The British Navy reporters (propagandists like all other military reporters of yesterday and today because they think it is their duty to lie as well as to kill for their country) then publish the news that the depraved mutineer Budd, who had stabbed and murdered a respected officer of the man-of-war, the H. M. S. *Indomitable*, has been convicted and executed for his dastardly crime, so that peace and harmony have been restored to His Majesty's indomitable *Indomitable*.

(Read *Billy Budd* in any of a dozen paperbound editions, or, with other shorter works in the paperbound volume, *The Shorter Novels of Herman Melville* [*Benito Cereno; The Encantadas, or Enchanted Isles; Bartleby the Scrivener;* and *Billy Budd, Foretopman*], with Introduction by Raymond Weaver, published by Fawcett Publications, Greenwich, Conn. Read also Melville's *Typee,* with Introduction by Clifton Fadiman; *The Confidence-Man: His Masquerade,* edited by Hennig Cohen; and *Israel Potter: Fifty Years of Exile.*)

Great Poets. The poets chosen for our core list of masterpieces are Homer, Vergil, Dante, Chaucer, Spenser, again the peerless Shakespeare, Milton, and Whitman. Their imperishable masterpieces, reflecting the spirit as well as the life and customs of the past, are known, loved, and admired in all lands. There are no substitutes for these fundamental works in every reader's personal library.

HOMER (ca. 800 or 900 B.C.), the world's first great storyteller, is assumed to have been the blind author of *The Iliad* and *The Odyssey,* the two Greek epics each of which presented in a single set of books the oral tales popular in the Western world three thousand years ago. The modern reader, like the ancients, is enchanted by the swift narrative, simple yet dignified language, and nobility and grandeur of Homer's works. These epic poems prove how little human beings have changed, how very little for the better, during the past three millennia. We see in them as we read the same confused mixture of hate and love, greed and nobility, violence and remorse, arrogance and humility, crime and punishment, truth and falsehood, stupidity and wisdom, evil and good universally familiar in all regions of the world today.

The Iliad tells about the most critical event in the Trojan War, about 1200 B.C. Paris, Prince of Troy, and guest of King Menelaus of Sparta, has run off with Helen, wife of the King, to Troy, and the Greeks in a thousand ships, led by King Agamemnon of Mycenae, brother of Menelaus, have sailed to bring Helen back. For more than nine years they have besieged Troy in vain. The story begins with a quarrel about women captives between Achilles, Greek hero and champion, and King Agamemnon. Proud Achilles shocks the Greeks by retiring to his tent and refusing to fight, but changes his mind when his dearest friend is slain by the Trojan prince Hector, and vows revenge. Homer describes the ferocious duel between Achilles and Hector, in which the Greek warrior finally hurls his spear straight into Hector's neck and then taunts the dying hero who begs to be sent home for a religious death ceremony: "Dog, you need not beg at my knees. Never will the mother who gave you life lay you out in death and mourn over you, but the dogs and birds, they will feast their fill on you." And after Hector dies, Achilles ties the body to his chariot and drags it in the dust before the Trojan multitude, as Hector's mother mourns and tears her hair at the sight, and his father groans pitifully, while Hector's noble widow Andromache, who had begged him not to fight, and the people of Troy weep bitterly at the loss of their mighty champion. At last, Achilles relents and surrenders the slain hero to his father, King Priam of Troy, for a ransom, and Hector is at last accorded the burial rites due to an honored hero.

(Read the translation by Richmond Lattimore in the paperbound volume, *The Iliad of Homer*, published by the University of Chicago Press, Chicago, Illinois. Other good translations are those by W. H. D. Rouse; by Andrew Lang, Walter Leaf, and Ernest Myers; by E. V. Rieu; and by Samuel Butler.)

The Odyssey, the world's most famous adventure story, tells about the exploits of the Greek warrior Odysseus during his years of wandering after the ten-year siege and conquest of Troy. An additional ten years were to pass before he could rejoin his son Telemachus and his faithful wife Penelope on their native island of Ithaca— ten years of battling against odds, against gods, storms and seas, cannibals and monsters, including the one-eyed Cyclops, Scylla the sea-devil, Charybdis the sea-sucker, and other fearsome creatures, while a hundred insolent suitors pester Penelope at home, telling her that Odysseus will never return and urging her to choose one of them for a husband. The traitors even plot to murder Telemachus. In the end the noble Odysseus, disguised as a beggar, joins his son in Ithaca, and they trap and kill the suitors, restoring peace to their household and their strife-torn land.

(There are a dozen fine translations of *The Odyssey* available in paperbound editions.)

VERGIL, PUBLIUS VERGILIUS MARO (70 B.C.–19 B.C.), next to Homer the most gifted poet of the ancient world, was inspired not only by Homer's work but by his own patriotic love of the Roman Empire, and the Emperor Augustus encouraged and befriended him. After composing two exquisite books of poetry extolling the peaceful country life of his age in Italy (in one, the ten charming, sensitive, separate poems of the *Eclogues*, which prophesied that a Saviour would come to purify the world, and in the other, the beautiful, rhythmic paean to farming and virtuous, glorious living in Italy, the fascinating *Georgics*—both fortunately combined and available now in excellent paperbound editions), Vergil devoted to his masterwork, the national epic *The Aeneid*, the last ten years of his lifetime.

The Aeneid, combining heroic adventures and romantic stories with patriotic and religious glorification of Rome, of Italy, and of the emperor Augustus, with its beautiful sound and rhythm and its alliteration, became a model poem for poets of succeeding ages, especially for Milton and Tennyson. After the conquest of Troy by the Greeks, the Trojan hero Aeneas escapes from the burning city with his men in twenty ships, reaching the palace of Queen Dido of Carthage who falls in love with the wandering hero. Aeneas tells Queen Dido how the Greeks had built a giant wooden horse, left it filled with soldiers in front of Troy, then sailed away, tricking the Trojans into opening the city gates and bringing the Trojan horse and soldiers into the city, where they were joined by the returning fleet and together slaughtered the Trojans. Thus fell the city of Troy at last. Aeneas continues the story of his escape from the burning city and his wanderings, ending with the death of his father Anchises.

Queen Dido begs Aeneas to remain in Carthage, not to desert her, but he feels that Fate, to him personified by the gods, compels him to leave for Italy. When he departs without showing her any tenderness or concern, the angry, brokenhearted, desperate Queen kills herself with her sword. Aeneas goes to Sicily where funeral games are held in his father's memory. He then sails to Latium in Italy, where King Latinus offers him his daughter Lavinia in marriage. But the queen Amata and Turnus, Lavinia's betrothed, condemn the proposed marriage, and civil war results, in which Aeneas kills Turnus in a duel. Thus it is the destiny of Dido to die despite her love for Aeneas, it is the destiny of Turnus to die despite his love for Lavinia, and it is the destiny of Aeneas and his descendants to lay the foundations of the Roman Empire.

(Read *The Aeneid*, packed with adventures, history, prophecies, deeds of evil and of justice, magical incidents, omens, strategies, romances, acts of duty and patriotism, journeys to Hades and to the Elysian Fields, triumphs and tragedies, wars and death, and, in the midst of war, a constant thirst for enduring peace, the Roman peace of the glorious Empire founded by Romulus and ruled by the great Augustus—read this ancient masterpiece which mirrors the world of humanity of yesterday and today, in any of a dozen excellent translations from the Latin, in paperbound editions, among which are translations by C. Day Lewis, W. J. Jackson Knight, Rolfe Humphries, Patric Dickinson, Kevin Guinagh, and James H. Mantinband.)

DANTE, ALIGHIERI (1265–1321), Florentine soldier, statesman, poet, artist, philosopher, inspired by his love of Beatrice to attain a higher, immortal, spiritual love, wrote in the musical, rhythmical Italian language *The New Life*, the story of his love for her, and then, after her death, devoted his lifetime to creating the most famous and influential masterpiece of the Middle Ages, *The Divine Comedy*.

The Divine Comedy (Dante called it simply *Commedia*, not *Commedia divina*) describes the destiny of human souls after death, in Hell, Purgatory, and Paradise; and the punishment of men for their evil deeds, or their rewards for good ones. The poem is in *terza rima*, a form of triple rhythm, in stanzas of three lines each, the second line of one stanza rhyming with the first and third lines of the next stanza. There are a hundred cantos in three parts: the *Inferno*, with thirty-four cantos; the *Purgatorio*, with thirty-three cantos, and the *Paradiso*, with thirty-three cantos. The rhythmic poetry reflects the ideas of Vergil and other Latin poets as well as those of the Hebrew prophets of the Old Testament.

The story tells how the thirty-five-year-old Dante is guided by Vergil's spirit (sent by the spirit of Dante's beloved lady Beatrice) out of the corrupt world of lustful, avaricious mankind into the Lord's "mountain of delight." They defy the power of obstructing beasts (leopard, lion, and she-wolf). They journey from the bleak plain of Anti-Hell (where the neutral souls, neither good nor evil, rush after a false banner throughout eternity) into Hell itself, populated by malicious, beastly, gluttonous, sinful souls. And so on, into the world of Limbo (with its virtuous heathens and unbaptized children); Upper Hell (with carnal, naked sinners who are whirled endlessly around and around in the darkness, the storms, the black mire, and mutual torture); into the city of eternal fire and intolerable stench; to the rivers of boiling blood where murderers, suicides, blasphemers, and the rich noblemen of Padua and Florence, the usurers and not the Jews, are cruelly tortured; and on and on through hellish depths, up, up to the world of Purgatory, inhabited by repentant and hopeful souls, to the place where Dante's beloved Beatrice (whose perfect ideals he had never attained) awaits, into the nine heavens of Paradise itself, where Beatrice leads Dante higher and higher into the realm of the angels with its divine light, beauty, peace, liberty, justice, piety, fortitude, truth, knowledge, eternal life, and supreme love which "moves the sun and the other stars" ("L'amor che move il sole e l'altre stelle.").

(A new three-volume bilingual prose edition of the Temple Classics edition of *The Divine Comedy* in English and Italian by J. H. Carlyle and others is available [E. P. Dutton, 1933, clothbound; Modern Library, 1950, paperbound; Random House Vintage Books, paperbound]. Another bilingual edition with the English translation in prose is that of J. D. Sinclair in three economical paperbound volumes, published by Oxford University Press. A translation of the first two parts [Inferno and Purgatorio] in verse by J. Ciardi is highly recommended.)

CHAUCER, GEOFFREY (ca. 1340–1400). Compassionate, humorous, cynical yet romantic poet, soldier, diplomat, and government official, Chaucer was the true father of English poetry. His works of genius picture for us the men and women, ideas, superstitions, and customs of all classes in his time—the lovers, knights, faithful and faithless women, sentimental warriors, physicians, parsons, monks, priests, and nuns, clerks, stewards, merchants, carpenters, millers, royal aristocrats, loud and coarse characters, adulterers, lawyers, country gentlemen and other gentle men, misers, fools and liars, serfs, kings, dreamers, astrologers, heroes, fakers, and rogues—every conceivable kind of character familiar in his age and ever since. Chaucer was himself a London townsman, endowed with common sense and a sense of humor, who loved country life as well and also journeyed to foreign lands, especially to Italy where he was influenced by and borrowed from the writings of Dante and those of the great contemporary authors Petrarch and Boccaccio. He painted people as they were, tolerant of the failings of men and women but telling the precise truth about them, making them seem so real and lifelike that we feel as if we have met each of them and know them well.

Chaucer's *Canterbury Tales*, by far his greatest work, is poetry created in an imaginative, ironic, sophisticated style, consisting of twenty-four fascinating stories, most of which are related in rhythmic, rhyming verse, by pilgrims to their companions on a pilgrimage from London to the shrine of Saint Thomas à Becket at Canterbury. The first two stories, *The Knight's Tale* and *The Miller's Tale*, illustrate the style and mood of all the rest.

The Knight's Tale is a tale of two Theban knights, lifelong friends, who, while in prison at Athens, see at a distance and fall in love with a beautiful, virtuous maiden, Emelye. One of the knights, Arcite, is released from prison on condition that he leave the region and never return. Thus, both knights are brokenhearted, for neither will be able to see their beloved Emelye again. But, after several years, Arcite, whose appearance has changed so much that he cannot be recognized, returns, and the other knight, Palamon, escapes from prison. The two knights are caught fighting a duel over their beautiful beloved, chaste Emelye, and the King of Athens orders them to be executed. The Queen and other ladies intercede to save the knights because, after all, they had made fools of themselves only through being in love. The tale ends with the accidental death of Arcite, who dies urging Emelye to love his worthy, gentle friend Palamon, saying that he, Arcite, would be "now in his colde grave alone, without any compaigne. Fare well, my sweete foo, myn

Emelye!" Thus, Palamon is left to marry the beautiful lady and cherish her forevermore in "parfit joye." So the fates, the gods, decree, for so the world is made, and we must all accept it as it is.

The Miller's Tale, told by the drunken miller, is about a wealthy old carpenter, married to Alisoun, a girl of eighteen ("Her mouth was sweete as bragot or the meeth," that is, sweet as honey and ale or mead) but they have a lustful boarder, the poor scholar Nicholas, who secretly loves Alisoun and tricks the stupid carpenter into sleeping on the roof in a tub because another Noah's flood is coming. As the two young lovers meet, another, the churchman Absalon, who also yearns to make love to Alisoun, stands at her window and begs for a kiss which she gives him on her extended buttocks, until he hears Nicholas laughing heartily inside the darkened room. Absalon, enraged, gets his revenge by placing a hot plowshare against Nicholas's bottom (also extended at the window to repeat Alisoun's trick), and amid the noise and confusion the carpenter and all the neighbors are awakened. So it comes about that the jealous old husband is twice deceived and the two lecherous young men are suitably punished, but Alisoun escapes the hot plowshare meant for her. (For young ladies like her, and for more virtuous ones, I recommend a book of musical poems, rhythmic, rhyming ditties, by Robert Warren, offering them wise counsel about the values of true love: *Facts of Wife,* published by Rodney Publishing Company, New York.)

(Read all the stories in the *Canterbury Tales,* for they are inimitable sources of pleasure. There are easy-to-read bilingual editions in paperbound format, as well as several interlinear and modern English versions. Read also Chaucer's *Troilus and Criseyde* in modern English verse by George Philip Krapp.)

SPENSER, EDMUND (1552?–1599), worthy successor to Chaucer and contemporary of Shakespeare, wrote exquisite, classical poetry admired as inspiring models by poets such as Milton, Keats, Burns, and Tennyson—

smoothly flowing, meditative poems in praise of friendship, love, beauty, joy, and truth, formal and dignified in tone, establishing what became known as the Spenserian stanza of nine lines, consisting of eight lines in iambic pentameter (weak-strong five-foot lines) and a ninth line in iambic hexameter (weak-strong six-foot line), created specially for use in his *Faerie Queen.*

The Faerie Queen, Spenser's best-known work, in six books (and a seventh unfinished) praises six of the twelve virtues advocated by Aristotle, all six combined in the great idealistic hero, Prince Arthur, that magnanimous gentleman, that "noble person in vertuous and gentle discipline," soon to become the renowned King Arthur.

Thus the first book is about *Holiness* and tells the story of the slaying of the devilish Dragon Errour (the "damned feend") by Georgos, the Redcrosse Knight (Saint George in later times) to liberate the castle of princess Una's father in the Kingdom of Eden. In Book II, Guyon, the knight of *Temperance,* captures Acrasia, the seductive, evil enchantress and is himself rescued from enemies by Prince Arthur. In Book III, a tribute to true love and *Chastity,* the heroine Britomart, guardian of purity in love, releases the virgin bride-to-be Amoret from the clutches of the evil magician Busyrane. Book IV, with its numerous suspenseful adventures, eulogizes loving *Friendship* and tells how quarrels among friends are settled by true friendship and peaceful affection, as in a good marriage. Book V tells of *Justice* being meted out by the fairy knight Artegall who judges like King Solomon in a murder case and saves the queen Irena from a wicked giant. Book VI praises *Courtesy* and the gentle tongue while telling the story of how the knight Calidore captures the slanderous monster, the Blatant Beast. Book VII, unfinished, has two cantos, praising stability and peace which will come (despite unhappy changes) to the land of glorious Queen Elizabeth, the "faerie queen."

(Read at least the paperbound volume, Edmund Spenser's *Faerie Queen; Books I and II, The Mutability Cantos,* and *Representative Minor Poems,* edited by Robert L. Kellogg and Oliver L. Steele, published by The Odyssey Press, Inc., New York.)

SHAKESPEARE, WILLIAM (1564–1616), in addition to the exquisite poetry of his peerless plays (see p. 151), wrote the most nearly perfect poems ever written, the *Sonnets,* in iambic pentameter (weak-strong five-foot lines), expressing deeply philosophical and sensitive, emotional, yet highly intellectual ideas, sentiments, and ideals, exploring his inner soul and relationships to his beloved dark lady, human destiny, hopes and fears, the wonders of man and nature.

But who can speak for Shakespeare better than Shakespeare? The following is a *Sonnet* (the Seventy-First) to his beloved:

> No longer mourn for me when I am dead
> Than you shall hear the surly sullen bell
> Give warning to the world that I am fled
> From this vile world, with vilest worms to dwell:
> Nay, if you read this line, remember not
> The hand that writ it; for I love you so
> That I in your sweet thoughts would be forgot
> If thinking on them then should make you woe.
> O, if I say, you look upon this verse
> When I perhaps compounded am with clay,
> Do not so much as my poor name rehearse,
> But let your love even with my life decay,
>   Lest the wise world should look into your moan
>   And mock you with me after I am gone.

(Read William Shakespeare, *Sonnets,* edited by Douglas Bush and Alfred Harbage, a paperbound volume published by Penguin Books, Inc., New York; or *The Sonnets, Songs, and Poems of William Shakespeare,* a paperbound volume edited by Oscar J. Campbell, published by Bantam Books, Inc., New York.)

MILTON, JOHN (1608–1674), author of heroic, religious, formal, musical, philosophical poems in blank verse (unrhymed verse), was a man of great ideals passionately devoted to human liberty and moral integrity. It was he who wrote the famous essay, *Areopagitica,* in defense of a free press more than three hundred years ago. He wrote those magnificent masterpieces of poetry, *Paradise Lost* and *Paradise Regained,* in his later years, when he was totally blind. His poetry, including the superb poetic drama *Samson Agonistes* (in a form based upon ancient Greek tragedies), pleaded eloquently for the cause of human freedom, humility, dignity, "virtue and public civility," condemning all forms of corruption, whether they be in politics or even in the church itself, and appealing at all times to the highest spiritual aims of man.

Paradise Lost tells in a grand style the grandest story of the contest between good and evil, Satan and the fall of man in the Garden of Eden, and the terrible punishment which inevitably results from wickedness and sin—the story

> Of Man's first Disobedience, and the Fruit
> Of that Forbidden Tree, whose mortal taste
> Brought Death into the World, and all our woe,
> With loss of Eden, till one greater Man
> Restore us, and regain the blissful Seat,
> Sing, heavenly muse, that on the secret top
> Of Oreb, or of Sinai, didst inspire
> That shepherd, who first taught the chosen seed,
> In the beginning, how the heavens and earth
> Rose out of chaos: . . .
> And justify the ways of God to men. (Book I, Invocation)

(Read *John Milton: Poems and Selected Prose,* a paperbound volume by Marjorie Nicholson, published by Bantam Books, Inc., New York; or *The Portable Milton: Paradise Lost, Paradise Regained, Samson Agonistes,* and *Comus,* edited by Douglas Bush, published in paperbound form by Viking Press, Inc., New York); or any of a number of other popular collections available in paperbound or clothbound editions.)

WHITMAN, WALT (1819–1892), pioneering creator of spontaneous, musical but irregular free verse, was a poetic seer, our foremost poet of democracy, who wrote the message of democracy, human brotherhood and mutual respect, which today gives us hope of a new society, for he taught us that society makes men what they are and men make society what it is.

> You felons on trial in courts,
> You convicts in prison-cells, you sentenced assassins
> Chained and hand-cuffed with iron,
> Who am I too that I am not on trial or in prison?
> Me, ruthless and devilish as any, that my wrists
>   are not chained with iron, or my ankles with iron?

In his masterwork, *Leaves of Grass,* Whitman inspired all men with his vision of a new freedom, a true democratic spirit, for no single nation, not the best or mightiest, can tell the whole story of the individual soul or shape the destiny of the race. So Whitman insisted upon telling the whole truth about American life—its virtues and its corruption, its dreams and its despair, but always ending with hope for the future of the Earth which "grows such sweet things out of such corruption, . . . It gives such divine materials to men, and accepts such leavings from them at last."

(Read Whitman's *Leaves of Grass* in any of a half-dozen paperbound editions, or in collections such as *The Portable Walt Whitman*, a paperbound volume edited by Mark Van Doren, published by Viking Press, Inc., New York. Among contemporary poets searching for a fresh approach to our own times, as Whitman did in his time, is Elie Siegel. Be sure to read his *Hail American Development*—containing 178 poems, including thirty-two translations from Catullus, Verlaine, Basho, Endre Ady, Martin Luther, La Fontaine, and Baudelaire—published in a revised paperbound edition, as well as a handsome clothbound edition by Definition Press, New York, in 1968.)

Great Satirists, Essayists, Critics, and Biographers. Every home library should contain representative works of the famous prose writers who influenced the minds of men and the shape of the modern world. The following indispensable works are available in paperbound editions.

PLUTARCH (46?–120 A.D.), Greek biographer, wrote *Parallel Lives* (about the lives of famous men), which was translated by Sir Thomas North in 1579–1603. The following paragraph is quoted from North's translation of *The Life of Julius Caesar* (from Walter W. Skeat, *Shakespeare's Plutarch,* London, 1875):

> Now Caesar immediately won many men's good will at Rome through his eloquence in pleading of their causes, and the people loved him marvelously also, because of the courteous manner he had to speak to every man, and to use them gently, being more ceremonious therein than was looked for in one of his years. Furthermore, he ever kept a good board, and fared well at his table, and was very liberal besides: the which indeed did advance him forward, and brought him in estimation with the people.

(Read the paperbound volume, *Plutarch's Lives of Nine Illustrious Greeks and Romans,* translated by John Dryden and Arthur H. Clough, edited by Wendell Clausen, published by Washington Square Press, Inc., New York.)

AUGUSTINE, SAINT (354–430 A.D.), great church philosopher, wrote *The City of God* and the autobiographical *Confessions. The City of God* blamed the destruction of Rome by the Goths (in 410 A.D.) upon the unwise faith of men in many gods and upon sinful living on earth, and envisioned the rise of another city in which all men could live in peace, with allegiance only to God— the City of God. The *Confessions* explains that the author had studied many philosophies and religions before choosing the path of Christian virtue, rejecting evil pleasures and disorderly systems of ideas.

(Read the *Confessions of Saint Augustine,* translated by John K. Ryan, and *The City of God* [abr.], edited by Vernon J. Bourke, both volumes published in paperbound editions by Doubleday & Co., New York.)

ERASMUS, DESIDERIUS (1466?–1536), native of Rotterdam, was a noted theologian and scholar, who attempted to reconcile his friend Luther's doctrines with those of the Catholic Church. He wrote his satire, *The Praise of Folly,* to expose the foolishness of the customs, beliefs, behavior, and institutions of mankind. We should praise, and be thankful for, universal folly, he said, because it succeeds so well in producing what exists today, namely, lazy people, drunks, warring nations, bigheaded (or pigheaded) persons, and stupid, arrogant men, and even perpetuates the race, for if men were wise, they would never think of marrying, of having children, or of keeping our mad world from collapsing. Give thanks to folly, for it is folly that fools foolish people into being the fools they are and doing the foolish things they do.

(Read *Essential Works of Erasmus*, edited by W. T. H. Jackson, a paperbound volume published by Bantam Books, Inc., New York.)

MONTAIGNE, MICHEL DE (1533–1592), French skeptic, wrote the *Essays*, consisting of ninety-four brilliant, frank, lucid, lively essays about human nature, its good and bad sides, being careful not to praise nor to condemn either himself or others, balancing virtues with vices and finding them all within himself: bravery and cowardice, egotism and humility, cruelty and remorse, the entire gamut of human contradictions and extremes of character.

(Read *The Complete Essays of Montaigne*, translated by Donald M. France, Jr., a paperbound volume published by Stanford University Press, Stanford, California; or *Selected Essays of Montaigne*, translated by John Florio, edited by Walter Kaiser, a paperbound volume published by Houghton Mifflin Co., Boston, Mass.)

SWIFT, JONATHAN (1667–1745), Irish-born writer of satire, wrote the masterpiece *Gulliver's Travels*, a fantastic tale, to dramatize the follies of society and the defects of human nature. The ship's surgeon, Lemuel Gulliver, tells the story of four amazing, imaginary adventures on journeys to four foreign lands. He bitterly attacks established institutions, including the Church, and even portrays men as lower and more fiendish than beasts. In one of his fantastic tales, despicable men become slaves to an intelligent community of horses, and the horses are so far superior to human beings that Gulliver can scarcely endure the sight of people when he returns to their evil civilization and compares them to the noble race of horses.

(Read *Gulliver's Travels* in any of fifteen good paperbound editions, which include *The Portable Swift,* edited by Carl Van Doren, published by Viking Press, New York.)

VOLTAIRE (FRANÇOIS MARIE AROUET) (1694–1778), the great French freethinker, wrote more than seventy volumes which disregarded conventional ideas and demanded with a very sharp, cynical, witty pen that men use their reason and the right of free speech to investigate and tell the truth about social institutions, literature, and religion. In *Candide,* which he wrote at the age of sixty-five years, he shows how accidents and calamities can upset human ambitions and he satirizes with savage irony the easy optimism of philosophers about this world as the best of all possible worlds. In his *Philosophical Letters,* he attacks contemporary institutions, including the futile French Academy, praises the influence of the British shopkeepers but condemns the literature of England for its disorder and lack of good taste. In his alphabetical *Philosophical Dictionary,* he expresses liberal, rational views on government, religion, and innumerable other topics in every field of human interest. He insists on complete separation between church and state, with the state in full control over social institutions and policies.

(Read *Candide* in any of numerous translations in paperbound volumes, including the bilingual edition translated by Lowell Bair, published by Bantam Books, Inc., New York; and *Philosophical Letters,* translated by Ernest N. Dilworth, published by Bobbs-Merrill Co., Inc., Indianapolis, Ind.)

JOHNSON, SAMUEL (1709–1784), author of the first great English dictionary (in two volumes, the model for all later dictionaries), the romantic, moralistic tale *Rasselas,* the remarkable work of masterly criticism, *Lives of the English Poets,* and numerous essays, poems, and plays, became the subject of the famous *Life of Samuel*

Johnson by James Boswell, one of the most entertaining, vivid, and admired biographies ever written. Johnson was by far the leading literary personality of his time, a master of words, the foremost and most influential conversationalist, a versatile literary giant unequaled to this day. Many definitions in his dictionary still remain valid two centuries later. The romantic novel *Rasselas* is a moralistic discussion of man's vanity and his vain search for happiness. *The Lives of the English Poets* contains penetrating critical opinions about the works of fifty-two poets, especially Milton, Swift, and Pope, delightful, spirited, inspiring biographical masterpieces. Boswell's *Life of Samuel Johnson* records Dr. Johnson's eloquent conversations (particularly those with associates in The Literary Club), anecdotes, and letters.

(Available in paperbound editions are: Johnson's *Rasselas, Poems and Selected Prose*, edited by Bertrand H. Bronson, published by Holt, Rinehart & Winston, Inc., New York; *Lives of the English Poets—Selections*, edited by Warren Fleischauer, published by Henry Regnery Co., Chicago, Ill.; and several editions of Boswell's *Life of Samuel Johnson*, including the original work edited by R. W. Chapman, published by Oxford University Press, New York.)

ROUSSEAU, JEAN JACQUES (1712–1778) was the philosophical giant of early modern philosophy of the state and pioneer in the history of education, intellectual godfather of the American Revolution, the French Revolution, and other revolutions, past and future, based on the ideas of human rights, democracy, and liberty. His radical, impassioned small book, *The Social Contract*, denounced monarchy and aristocracy of any kind and demanded their destruction by the only means then possible—revolution—and advocated a new political and social order controlled by and for the common people, the key to which is rule by majority vote, by enlightened, free majorities. Rousseau was Jefferson's teacher by proxy of *The Social Contract* and therefore the true spiritual founder of American democracy, to whom too little credit or appreciation has been shown by Americans. His masterpiece *Émile* is probably the most influential, inspiring, and sound book on education ever written, the foundation for every decent trend in modern education, pleading for the study of nature, learning by doing, thinking, and living co-operatively with one's fellow human beings, with respect for the individual's abilities, desires, and psychological needs. His pioneering book *Confessions* laid bare his own emotional life, including his affairs with women, and set a precedent for all future investigations and writings about the psychology of sex and human relationships.

(Read these indispensable books by Rousseau in paperbound editions: *The Social Contract,* edited by Charles Frankel, published by Hafner Publishing Co., New York; *The Émile of Jean Jacques Rousseau,* translated by William Byrd, published by Teachers College Press, Columbia University, New York; and Rousseau, Jean-Jacques, *The Confessions,* translated by J. M. Cohen, published by Penguin Books, Inc., New York.)

EMERSON, RALPH WALDO (1803–1882), New England's visionary poet, essayist, radical in religion, and critic, wrote in behalf of fundamental American ideals of his time—self-realization, self-reliance, independence of spirit, hope in the future of each human being, subordination of the state to the individual citizen (the less government we have, the better, he said), toleration of differences in opinion and religion, social change to achieve noble ideals—and he expressed these ideas in all his poems, essays, and lectures.

(Read any of a dozen collections of Emerson's writings available in paperbound form, including such collections as: *The Portable Emerson,* edited by Mark Van Doren, published by The Viking Press, Inc. New York); or Ralph Waldo Emerson, *Selected Prose and Poetry,* edited by Reginald L. Cook, published by Holt, Rinehart & Winston, New York.)

THOREAU, HENRY DAVID (1817–1862), another New England visionary poet and essayist, carried Emerson's individualism into practical affairs by refusing for six years to pay his taxes, and accepting a night's imprisonment as penalty in protest against slavery and the Fugitive Slave Law. In his revolutionary essay, *Civil Disobedience,* Thoreau explained that the citizen has a duty to resist any government which accepts or helps preserve immoral institutions such as slavery. His principles had great influence on Mahatma Gandhi and thus eventually resulted in the liberation of India from British rule. Thoreau lived as a hermit in a hut for months at Walden Pond, in Massachusetts, where he planned his famous book, *Walden,* extolling the simple life (and man's search for his own fulfillment as part of nature) in preference to the trappings, restraints, and artificiality of society.

(Thoreau wrote many poems, reflecting his personal experiences and independence of mind, as well as travel books, including: *A Week on the Concord and Merrimack Rivers,* edited by Walter Harding, paperbound, published by Holt, Rinehart & Winston, New York; *Cape Cod* and *The Maine Woods,* both paperbound volumes published by Apollo Editions, Inc., New York. Numerous editions of his classic *Walden* are available in paperbound form; a good sourcebook is *Thoreau: Walden and Other Writings,* edited by Joseph Wood Krutch, published by Bantam Books, Inc., New York.)

9

Special Books in Literature, Philosophy, Psychology, Religion, Science, and The Arts

In the spiritual house of learning, there are millions of living voices, books created in the past three thousand years representing the thoughts and feelings of countless generations of human beings who labored to fashion these treasures, ever growing sources of inspiration and knowledge for our and future generations. Indispensable foundation books have been named in the preceding pages. The books listed below comprise significant additional contributions by creative minds to several branches of the glorious tree of knowledge: literature, philosophy, psychology, religion, science, and the arts.

Most highly recommended for everyone's home library are the works of those authors whose names are printed in **bold type**. For the first time in history, nearly all of these books are available in economical, paperbound editions so that millions of readers can obtain them. Many of them are also published in attractive clothbound editions. For information about the publishers and prices, consult *Books in Print* and *Paperbound Books in Print,* both published by R. R. Bowker Company, 1180 Avenue of the Americas, New York, N.Y. 10036. These guidebooks can be found readily in most bookstores and libraries.

Aesop (6th century B.C.). *Fables,* translated by S. A. Handford.

Addison, Joseph (1672–1719) and Steele, Sir Richard (1672–1729). *Selections from the Tatler and the Spectator,* edited by R. J. Allen.

Aiken, Conrad (1889–   ). *Selected Poems. Collected Short Stories.*

Albee, Edward (1928–   ). *Who's Afraid of Virginia Woolf? Ballad of the Sad Café.*

Alcott, Louisa May (1832–1880). *Little Women.*

Aleichem, Sholom (Solomon Rabinovitz) (1859–1916). *The Tevye Stories and Others. Adventures of Mottel the Cantor's Son. Great Fair: Scenes from My Childhood.*

Andersen, Hans Christian (1805–1875). *The Snow Queen. The Owl and the Pussy Cat.*

Anderson, Maxwell (1880–   ). *Four Verse Plays (Elizabeth the Queen, High Tor, Winterset, and Mary of Scotland).*

Anderson, Sherwood (1876–1941). *Winesburg, Ohio. Short Stories.*

Anouilh, Jean (1910–   ). *Becket. Five Plays.*

Apollinaire, Guillaume (1880–1918). *Alcools: Poems 1889?–1913. The Cubist Painters.*

Apollonius of Rhodes (late 3rd century B.C.). *The Voyage of Argo.*

Apuleius (2nd century A.D.). *The Golden Ass.*

Aquinas, Saint Thomas (1225?–1274). *On the Truth of the Catholic Faith,* 4 vols. *Philosophical Texts.*

Arabian Nights, The (ca. 900–1500). Anonymous. Translated by Richard F. Burton.

Archimedes (287–212 B.C.). *Works,* edited by T. L. Heath.

Ariosto, Lodovico (1474–1533). *Orlando Furioso,* translated by Sir John Harrington.

Aristotle (384–322 B.C.). *Ethics. Metaphysics. Poetics. Politics. The Rhetoric of Aristotle.*

Arnold, Matthew (1822–1888). *The Portable Matthew Arnold. Culture and Anarchy.*

Auden, Wystan Hugh (1907–   ). *Poems. For the Time Being. The Age of Anxiety.*

Aurelius, Marcus (121–180). *Meditations.*

Austen, Jane (1775–1817). *Emma. Pride and Prejudice. Mansfield Park. Sense and Sensibility. Persuasion.*

Babbitt, Irving (1865–1933). *Rousseau and Romanticism.*

Bacon, Francis (1561–1626). *New Organon. The Advancement of Learning. The New Atlantis.*

Balzac, Honoré de (1799–1850). *Père Goriot,* translated by M. A. Crawford. *Cousin Bette,* translated by M. A. Crawford. *Eugénie Grandet,* translated by Henry Reed.

Barrie, Sir James (1860–1937). *Peter Pan.*

Baudelaire, Charles Pierre (1821–1867). *Flowers of Evil,* translated by George Dillon and Edna St. Vincent Millay.

Beaumarchais, Pierre-Augustin Caron de (1732–1799). *The Marriage of Figaro* and *The Barber of Seville,* both translated by John Wood, Jr.

Becket, Samuel (1906–   ). *Waiting for Godot. Poems in English.*

Bellamy, Edward (1850–1898). *Looking Backward.*

Bellow, Saul (1915–   ). *The Adventures of Augie March. Herzog. Henderson the Rain King. Seize the Day.*

Benét, Stephen Vincent (1898–1942). *Selected Poetry and Prose.*

Bentham, Jeremy (1748–1832). *An Introduction to the Principles of Morals and Legislation.*

Beowulf (ca. 8th century A.D.). Anonymous. Translated by David Wright.

Bergson, Henri (1859–1941). *Creative Evolution.*

Berkeley, George (1685–1753). *Berkeley's Philosophical Writings.*

Bible, The Holy. Old Testament. New Testament.

Blake, William (1757–1827). *Songs of Innocence. Songs of Experience.*

Boccaccio, Giovanni (1313–1375). *Decameron. Fates of Illustrious Men.*

Boethius, Anicius Manlius Serverinus (480?–?524). *Consolation of Philosophy.*

Boileau (Despreaux), Nicolas (1636–1711). *Selected Criticism.*

Bolt, Robert (1924–   ). *A Man for All Seasons.*

Boole, George (1815–1864). *Laws of Thought.*

Boswell, James (1740–1795). *The Life of Samuel Johnson.*

Brecht, Bertolt (1898–1956). *Mother Courage. Galileo. Jungle of Cities and Other Plays.*

Brontë, Charlotte (1816–1855). *Jane Eyre.*

Brontë, Emily (1818–1848). *Wuthering Heights.*

Brooks, Van Wyck (1886–   ). *Flowering of New England. Ordeal of Mark Twain.*

Browning, Elizabeth Barrett (1806–1861). *Sonnets from the Portuguese.*

Browning, Robert (1812–1899). *The Ring and the Book.*

Bryant, William Cullen (1794–1878). *Selections,* edited by Samuel Sillen.

Bunyan, John (1628–1688). *Pilgrim's Progress.*

Burke, Edmund (1729–1797). *Reflections on the Revolution in France.*

Burns, Robert (1759–1796). *Selected Prose and Poetry of Robert Burns,* edited by Robert E. Thornton.

Butler, Samuel (1835–1902). *The Way of All Flesh.*

Byron, George Gordon (Lord) (1788–1824). *Don Juan. Selected Poetry and Prose of George Gordon Byron,* edited by W. H. Auden.

Caesar, Gaius Julius (100 B.C.–44 B.C.). *The Gallic Wars and Other Writings,* translated by Moses Hadas.

Calderon de la Barca, Pedro (1600–1681). *Four Plays,* translated by Edwin Honig.

Calvin, John (1509–1564). *On the Christian Faith (Selections from the Institutes, Commentaries, and Tracts).*

Camus, Albert (1913–1960). *The Plague. Stranger.*

Čapek, Karel (1890–1938). *R. U. R.*

Carlyle, Thomas (1795–1881). *Past and Present.*

Carroll, Lewis (Dodgson, Charles L., 1832–1898). *Alice in Wonderland. Nonsense Verse.*

Cary, Joyce (1888–1957). *The Horse's Mouth. Charley Is My Darling.*

Castiglione, Baldassar (1478–1529). *Book of the Courtier.*

Cather, Willa (1875–1947). *My Antonia.*

Catullus, Gaius Valerius (ca. 84–54 B.C.). *Poems of Catullus,* translated by Peter Wigham.

Cellini, Benvenuto (1500–1571). *Autobiography of Benvenuto Cellini,* translated by J. A. Symonds.

Chateaubriand, François René de (1768–1848). *Atala,* translated by Walter J. Cobb.

Chekhov, Anton (1860–1904). *Six Plays of Chekhov,* translated by R. W. Corrigan.

Chesterton, Gilbert Keith (1874–1906). *The Man Who Was Thursday.*

Cicero, Marcus Tullius (106–43 B.C.). *On the Commonwealth,* translated by G. H. Sabine and S. B. Smith. *On Old Age,* and *On Friendship,* both essays translated by H. G. Edinger.

Clausewitz, Karl von (1780–1831). *War, Politics, and Power.*

Cocteau, Jean (1891–1963). *The Infernal Machine and Other Plays.*

Coleridge, Samuel Taylor (1772–1834). *Coleridge: Poetry and Prose,* edited by Carlos Baker.

Collins, William Wilkie (1824–1889). *The Women in White. The Moonstone.*

Confucius (ca. 551–479 B.C.). *Analects of Confucius.*

Congreve, William (1670–1729). *The Way of the World.*

Conrad, Joseph (1857–1924). *Lord Jim. Nostromo. The Nigger of the Narcissus.*

Cooper, James Fenimore (1789–1851). *The Last of the Mohicans. The Pathfinder. The Deerslayer.*

Corneille, Pierre (1606–1684). *The Cid,* translated by R. Feltenstein.

Cozzens, James Gould (1903–   ). *Last Adam. The Just and the Unjust.*

Crane, Hart (1899–1932). *The Complete Poems and Selected Letters and Prose of Hart Crane*, edited by Brom Weber.
Crane, Stephen (1871–1900). *The Red Badge of Courage. Stories and Tales.*

Dalton, John (1766–1844). *New System of Chemical Philosophy.*
Descartes, René (1596–1650). *Meditations. Discourse on Method.*
De Quincey, Thomas (1785–1859). *Confessions of an English Opium-Eater.*
Dewey, John (1859–1952). *Democracy and Education. Experience and Nature.*
Dickinson, Emily Elizabeth (1839–1886). *Selected Poems and Letters.*
Diderot, Denis (1713–1784). *Rameau's Nephew. Encyclopedia Selections.*
Donne, John (1573–1631). *Selected Poems*, edited by John Hayward.
Dos Passos, John Roderigo (1896–   ). *U. S. A. The 42nd Parallel. Manhattan Transfer.*
Dostoievski, Fedor Mikhailovich (1821–1881). *The Brothers Karamazov. Crime and Punishment. The Idiot.*
Doyle, Arthur Conan (1859–1930). *The Adventures of Sherlock Holmes.*
Dreiser, Theodore (1871–1945). *An American Tragedy. Sister Carrie. The Financier.*
Dumas, Alexandre (1802–1870). *The Count of Monte Cristo.*
Durrell, Lawrence (1912–   ). *Balthazar. Justine. Poetry of Lawrence Durell.*

Einstein, Albert (1879–1955). *Relativity, the Special and General Theory. The Meaning of Relativity.*
Eliot, George (Mary Ann Evans) (1819–1880). *Adam Bede. Middlemarch. Silas Marner. The Mill on the Floss.*
Eliot, Thomas Stearns (1888–1965). *The Sacred Wood.*

*The Waste Land and Other Poems. Murder in the
Cathedral.*
Ellis, Havelock (1859–1939). *The Psychology of Sex.*
Epictetus (First century A.D.). *Moral Discourses,* trans-
lated by Carter-Higginson, edited by Thomas Gould.
Euclid (ca. 330–275 B.C.). *Elements.*

Farrell, James T. (1904–   ). *Studs Lonigan.*
Faulkner, William (1897–1962). *The Portable Faulkner,*
edited by Malcolm Cowley.
Fielding, Henry (1707–1754). *Tom Jones. Joseph An-
drews. Amelia.*
Fitzgerald, F. Scott (1896–1940). *The Fitzgerald Reader.
The Great Gatsby. Tender Is the Night.*
Flaubert, Gustave. *Madame Bovary. Sentimental Educa-
tion. Three Tales.*
Forster, Edward Morgan (1879–   ). *Passage to India.
The Longest Journey. Room with a View.*
Francis of Assisi, Saint (1181–1226). *Little Flowers of
Saint Francis,* translated by Leo Sherley-Price.
Franklin, Benjamin (1706–1790). *Autobiography. Benja-
min Franklin Papers.*
Frazer, Sir James G. *The New Golden Bough,* abridged,
edited by Theodor Gaster.
Freud, Sigmund (1856–1931). *The Psychopathology of
Everyday Life. On Dreams. An Outline of Psychoanaly-
sis. On Creativity and the Unconscious.*
Frost, Robert (1876–1963). *Robert Frost's Poems.*
Fuentes, Carlos (1929–   ). *The Death of Artemio
Cruz,* translated by S. Hileman.

Galilei, Galileo (1564–1642). *Dialogues Concerning The
Two Chief World Systems. Dialogues Concerning Two
New Sciences.*
Galsworthy, John (1867–1933). *Man of Property. The
Apple Tree and Other Tales.*
Genêt, Jean (1910–   ). *The Blacks,* translated by Ber-
nard Frechtman.
George, Henry (1837–1897). *Progress and Poverty.*

Gibbon, Edward (1737–1794). *The Portable Gibbon: The Decline and Fall of the Roman Empire*, edited by Dero A. Saunders.

Gide, André (1869–1951). *Journals, Vols. I and II. Strait is the Gate. Lafcadio's Adventures. Dostoevsky*, with Introduction by Albert Guerard. *Montaigne. Marshlands* and *Prometheus Misbound*, translated by George D. Painter.

Giraudoux, Jean (1882–1944). *Three Plays*, translated by Phyllis La Farge and Peter Judd.

Glasgow, Ellen (Ellen Anderson Gholson) (1874–1945). *Barren Ground. The Collected Stories of Ellen Glasgow*, edited by Richard K. Meeker. *Vein of Iron*.

Goethe, Johann Wolfgang von (1749–1832). *Faust*, bilingual edition translated by Walter Kaufmann. *Hermann and Dorothea*, translated by Daniel Coogan. *Götz von Berlichingen*, translated by Charles E. Passage. *The Sorrows of Young Werther*, bilingual edition, edited by Harry Steinhauer. *Torquato Tasso*, translated by Charles E. Passage. *Wilhelm Meister's Apprenticeship*, translated by Thomas Carlyle.

Gogol, Nicolai (1809–1852). *Dead Souls. Evenings Near the Village of Dikanka. The Inspector General. Overcoat and Other Tales of Good and Evil.*

Golding, William (1911–   ). *Lord of the Flies. The Inheritors. Pincher Martin. Free Fall. The Spire.*

Goldsmith, Oliver (1728–1774). *Four Plays*, edited by George Pierce Baker. *The Vicar of Wakefield. The Citizen of the World.*

Gorky, Maxim (1868–1936). *The Lower Depths and Other Plays*, translated by Alexander Bakshy and Paul S. Nathan. *Reminiscences* of *Tolstoy, Chekhov, and Andreyev*, Introduction by Mark van Doren.

Graves, Robert (1895–   ). *Collected Poems. Good-bye to All That. I, Claudius.*

Greene, Graham (1904–   ). *Brighton Rock. The Power and the Glory. The Heart of the Matter. A Burnt-Out Case. The Quiet American. Loser Takes All. Twenty-One Stories.*

Grimmelshausen, Hans Jakob Christoffel von (1620?–1676). *The Adventures of a Simpleton.*

Grotius, Hugo (1583–1645). *Prolegomena to the Law of War and Peace,* translated by Francis W. Kelsey.

Hamsun, Knut (1859–1952). *Pan.*

Hardy, Thomas (1840–1928). *Far from the Madding Crowd. Jude the Obscure. The Mayor of Casterbridge. The Return of the Native. Tess of the D'Urbervilles.*

Harte, Bret (1836–1902). *The Luck of Roaring Camp and Other Sketches.*

Harvey, William (1578–1657). *On the Motion of the Heart and Blood.*

Hauptmann, Gerhart (1862–1946). *Five Plays by Gerhaupt Hauptmann,* translated by Theodore Lustig, Introduction by John Gassner.

Hawthorne, Nathaniel (1804–1864). *The Scarlet Letter. The House of Seven Gables. The Blithedale Romance. The Marble Faun. Twice-Told Tales.*

Hegel, Georg Wilhelm Friedrich (1770–1831). *Lectures on the Philosophy of History,* translated by J. Silbree.

Heine, Heinrich (1797–1856). *Religion and Philosophy in Germany,* translated by John Snodgrass. *Buch der Lieder.*

Hellman, Lillian (1905–   ). *Six Plays,* in Modern Library.

Hemingway, Ernest (1898–1961). *A Farewell to Arms. For Whom The Bell Tolls. To Have and Have Not. The Old Man and the Sea. The Snows of Kilimanjaro and Other Stories.*

Herder, Johann Gottfried (1774–1803). *God, Some Conversations,* translated by Frederick H. Burkhardt.

Herodotus (ca. 484–425 B.C.). *History of the Greek and Persian War,* translated by George Rawlinson.

Hersey, John (1914–   ). *A Bell for Adano. Here To Stay,* including *Hiroshima. The Wall.*

Hobbes, Thomas (1588–1679). *Leviathan. Selections,* edited by Frederick E. Woodbridge.

Hochhuth, Rolf (1931–   ). *The Deputy*, translated by C. and R. Winston.

Hölderlin, Friedrich (1770–1843). *Hyperion. Selected Verse*, edited by Michael Hamburger.

Hopkins, Gerard Manley (1884–1889). *A Hopkins Reader*, edited by John Pick.

Horace (Quintus Horatius Flaccus) (65–8 B.C.). *Odes and Epodes of Horace*, translated by Joseph P. Clancy. *Satires and Epistles of Horace*, translated by Smith Palmer Bovie.

Housman, Alfred Edward (A. E.) (1859–1936). *A Shropshire Lad. Selected Prose*, edited by John Carter.

Howells, William Dean (1837–1920). *A Modern Instance. The Rise of Silas Lapham. The Hazard of New Fortunes*.

Hugo, Victor (1802–1885). *The Hunchback of Notre Dame. Les Miserables. Three Plays by Victor Hugo*, edited by Helen A. Gaubert.

Hume, David (1711–1776). *Essential Works of David Hume*, edited by Ralph Cohen.

Huxley, Aldous (1894–1963). *Brave New World. Collected Essays of Aldous Huxley. Grey Eminence. Antic Hay* and *The Gioconda Smile*, Introduction by Martin Green.

Ionesco, Eugene (1912–   ). *The Bald Soprano* in *Four Plays*, translated by Donald Mallen. *Notes and Counter-Notes*, translated by Donald Watson.

Irving, Washington (1783–1859). *The Sketch Book. A History of New York. The Legend of Sleepy Hollow. Selected Prose*, edited by S. T. Williams.

Isherwood, Christopher (1904–   ). *The Berlin Stories. Vedanta for the Western World. Down There on a Visit*.

James, Henry (1843–1916). *The Ambassadors. The Portrait of a Lady. The Great Short Stories of Henry James*, edited by Philip Rahv. *Washington Square. Selected Literary Criticism*, edited by Morris Shapera.

James, William (1842–1912). *Will to Believe and Human*

Immortality. Pragmatism and Other Essays, Introduction by Joseph L. Blau. *Psychology: The Briefer Course,* Introduction by Gordon Allport.

Jonson, Ben (1573–1637). *Three Plays, Vol. I; Three Plays, Vol. II;* both edited by Brinsley Nicholson and C. H. Herford.

Josephus, Flavius (37?–100). *The Jewish War and Other Selections from Flavius Josephus,* translated by H. St. J. Thackeray and Ralph Marcus.

Joyce, James (1882–1941). *Finnegan's Wake. The Portable James Joyce,* edited by Harry Levin.

Juvenal (Decimus Junius Juvenalis) (60?–?140 A.D.). *The Satires of Juvenal,* translated by Rolfe Humphries.

Kafka, Franz (1883–1926). *Amerika,* translated by Edwin Muir. *Parables and Paradoxes. The Penal Colony.*

Kant, Immanuel (1724–1804). *Critique of Pure Reason. Selections,* edited by Theodore M. Greene. *Groundwork of the Metaphysic of Morals,* translated by H. J. Paton.

Keats, John (1795–1821). *Complete Poetry and Selected Prose,* edited by Harold E. Briggs.

Keynes, John Maynard (1883–1946). *The General Theory of Employment, Interest, and Money. A Treatise on Probability. Essays on Persuasion.*

Kipling, Rudyard (1865–1936). *Captains Courageous. The Jungle Books. Kim. Just So Stories. A Choice of Kipling's Verse,* edited by T. S. Eliot.

Kleist, Heinrich von (1777–1811). *The Broken Jug,* translated by John T. Krumpelmann. *The Prince of Homburg,* translated by Charles E. Passage. *Amphitryon,* translated by Marion Sonnenfeld.

La Fontaine, Jean de (1621–1695). *The Fables of La Fontaine,* translated by Marianne Moore.

Lagerlöf, Selma (1858–1940). *The Story of Gösta Berling.*

Lamb, Charles (1775–1834). *The Portable Charles Lamb,* edited by John Mason Brown.

La Rochefoucauld, François (1747–1827). *The Maxims.*

Lawrence, D.H. (1885–1930). *The Complete Short Stories*

of D. H. Lawrence, 3 vols. *Four Short Novels. Lady Chatterley's Lover. Women in Love. Selected Literary Criticism*, edited by Anthony Beal. *The Rainbow*, Introduction by Richard Aldington.

Leibniz, Gottfried Wilhelm (1646–1716). *Selections*, edited by Philip P. Weiner. *Discourse on Metaphysics*, translated by George Montgomery.

Lenin, Nikolai (Vladimir Ilich Ulyanov) (1870–1924). *Essential Works of Lenin*, edited by Henry Christman. *What Is To Be Done? Teachings of Karl Marx.*

Lessing, Gotthold Ephraim (1729–1781). *Emilia Galotti*, translated by Edward Dvoretsky. *Laocoön*, translated by E. A. McCormick. *Nathan the Wise*, translated by Bayard Quincy Morgan.

Lewis, C. S. (1898–1963). *That Hideous Strength. Out of the Silent Planet. Perelandra. The Great Divorce.*

Lewis, Sinclair (1885–1951). *Arrowsmith. Dodsworth. Main Street. Elmer Gantry. Babbitt. Cass Timberlane. Kingsblood Royal.*

Lewis, Wyndham (1882–1957). *The Apes of God. Self Condemned.*

Lincoln, Abraham (1809–1865). *Selected Speeches, Messages, and Letters*, edited by T. Harry Williams.

Livy (Titus Livius) (59 B.C.–17 A.D.). *The Early History of Rome*, translated by Aubrey de Selincourt. *The War with Hannibal.*

Locke, John (1632–1704). *Locke's Essay Concerning Human Understanding*, 2 vols., edited by Alexander Campbell Fraser. *Treatise of Civil Government* and *A Letter Concerning Toleration*, edited by Charles L. Sherman. *John Locke on Education*, edited by Peter Gay.

London, Jack (1876–1916). *The Sea Wolf. Great Short Works of Jack London*, edited by Earl Labor. *Martin Eden.*

Longfellow, Henry Wadsworth (1807–1882). *The Essential Longfellow*, edited by Lewis Leary.

Lope de Vega (1562–1635). *Five Plays*, translated by Jill Booty.

Lorca, Federico Garcia (1899–1936). *Three Tragedies,* translated by Richard O'Connell and James Graham Lujan.

Lowell, Robert (1917–   ). *Imitations. The Old Glory* (including Benito Cereno, etc.).

Lucian (2nd century B.C.). *Selected Satires,* translated by B. F. Reardon.

Lucretius (Titus Lucretius Carus) (96?–55 B.C.). *On Nature,* translated by Russel M. Geer.

Luther, Martin (1483–1546). *Martin Luther: Selections from His Writings,* edited by John Dillenberger.

Macaulay, Rose (1881–1958). *The Towers of Trebizond.*

Macaulay, Thomas Babington. *Critical and Historical Essays,* edited by H. R. Trevor-Roper.

Machiavelli, Niccolò (1469–1527). *The Prince and Other Works,* translated by Luigi Ricci, Introduction by Max Lerner.

MacLeish, Archibald (1892–   ). *The Collected Poems of Archibald MacLeish.*

Maeterlinck, Maurice (1862–1949). *The Intruder,* in *Five Modern Plays* (*The Dreamy Kid* by Eugene O'Neill; *The Farewell Supper* by Arthur Schnitzler; *The Lost Silk Hat* by Lord Dunsany; *The Sisters' Tragedy* by Richard Hughes; and *The Intruder* by Maurice Maeterlinck, edited by Edmund R. Brown.) *The Blue Bird.*

Mailer, Norman (1923–   ). *The Naked and the Dead. Barbary Shore. The Deer Park.*

Maimonides (Rabbi Moses Ben Maimon, or RaM-BaM) (1135–1204). *Guide for the Perplexed,* translated by M. Friedlander. *Preservation of Youth.*

Malamud, Bernard (1914–   ). *The Assistant. Idiots First. The Magic Barrel. The Natural. A New Life.*

Mallarmé, Stephanie. *Selected Poems* (bilingual edition), translated by C. F. MacIntyre.

Malory, Sir Thomas (ca. 1470). *Le Morte d'Arthur: King Arthur and the Knights of the Round Table,* by Keith Baines, Introduction by Robert Graves.

Malraux, André (1901–   ). *The Conquerors. Man's Fate. The Royal Way.*

Malthus, Thomas Robert (1766–1834). *Population: the First Essay.*

Mann, Thomas (1875–1955). *Buddenbrooks. Death in Venice and Seven Other Stories. The Transposed Heads.*

Manzoni, Alessandro (1785–1873). *Betrothed* (*I Promessi Sposi*), translated by Archibald Colquhoun.

Maritain, Jacques (1882–   ). *Art and Scholasticism and The Frontiers of Poetry. A Preface to Metaphysics. The Range of Reason. Saint Thomas Aquinas.*

Marlowe, Christopher (1564–1593). *Complete Plays of Christopher Marlowe,* edited by Irving Ribner.

Marquand, John P. (1893–   ). *The Late George Apley. Wickford Point. Point of No Return. Repent in Haste. The Last of Mr. Moto.*

Martial (ca. 40–104). *Martial: Selected Epigrams,* translated by Rolfe Humphries.

Marx, Karl (1818–1883). *Das Kapital* (abr.). *Early Writings,* translated and edited by T. B. Bottomore. *Selected Writings in Sociology and Social Philosophy.* Marx and Engels, *Basic Writings on Politics and Philosophy,* edited by Lewis S. Feuer.

Maugham, W. Somerset (1847–1966). *Cakes and Ale. Moon and Sixpence. Of Human Bondage. The Razor's Edge.*

Maupassant, Guy de (1850–1893). *Portable Maupassant,* edited by Lewis Galantiere.

Mauriac, François (1885–   ). *The Lamb. Woman of the Pharisees,* translated by Gerard Hopkins. *Thérèse* (*Thérèse Desqueyroux*).

Maurois, André (Émile Salomon Wilhelm Herzog) (1885–   ). *Ariel: The Life of Shelley. Atmosphere of Love,* translated by Joseph Collins. *Byron.*

Mencken, Henry Louis (1880–1956). *Prejudice: A Selection,* edited by James T. Farrell. *Treatise on the Gods. Vintage Mencken,* edited by Alistair Cooke.

Meredith, George (1829–1909). *The Egoist. The Ordeal of Richard Feverel.*

Middleton, Thomas (1570?–1627). *A Mad World, My Masters. Michaelmas Term. The Changeling* (with William Rowley).

Mill, John Stuart (1806–1873). *Autobiography. Essential Works of John Stuart Mill,* edited by Max Lerner.

Millay, Edna St. Vincent (1892–1950). *Collected Sonnets of Edna St. Vincent Millay. Collected Lyrics of Edna St. Vincent Millay. The Letters of Edna St. Vincent Millay,* edited by Allan Ross MacDougall.

Miller, Arthur (1915–   ). *The Crucible. Death of a Salesman. Focus. Incident at Vichy. A View from the Bridge.*

Montesquieu, Charles de (1689–1755). *The Persian Letters. The Spirit of the Laws.*

Moore, Brian (1921–   ). *The Emperor of Ice-Cream.*

Moore, George (1852–1933). *Confessions of a Young Man. Esther Waters,* edited by Lionel Stevenson. *Mummer's Wife.*

Moore, George E. (1873–   ). *Philosophical Studies. Principia Ethica.*

Moore, Marianne Craig (1887–   ). *The Marianne Moore Reader.*

More, Sir Thomas (1478–1535). *Utopia,* translated by Peter K. Marshall.

Murdoch, Iris (1919–   ). *Under the Net. The Bell. The Flight from the Enchanter. A Severed Head. The Unicorn.*

Musset, Alfred de (1810–1857). *Seven Plays,* translated by Peter Meyers.

Nerudo, Pablo (1904–   ). *Selected Poems* (bilingual), translated by Luis Monguio.

Newton, Sir Isaac (1642–1727). *Newton's Philosophy of Nature,* edited by H. S. Thayer. *Principia, Vols. I and II. Optics.*

Nietzsche, Friedrich (1844–1900). *The Portable Nietzsche,* edited by Walter Kaufmann. *Thus Spake Zarathustra,* translated by R. J. Hollingdale. *Unpublished Letters. Use and Abuse of History,* translated by Adrian Collins.

O'Casey, Sean (1884–1964). *Drums under the Window.*
Five One-Act Plays. Three Plays. Three More Plays. I
Knock at the Door.

Odets, Clifford (1906–1963). *Six Plays. Golden Boy* (with
William Gibson).

O'Neill, Eugene (1888–1953). *Nine Plays. The Iceman*
Cometh. The Emperor Jones.

Orwell, George (Eric Blair, 1903– 1950). *Burmese Days.*
Animal Farm. Nineteen Eighty–Four, edited by Irving
Howe. *The Orwell Reader.*

Ovid (Publius Ovidius Naso) (ca. 43 B.C.–17 A.D.).
Metamorphoses, translated by Rolfe Humphries. *Art*
of Love. Love Poems of Ovid, translated by Horace
Gregory.

Pascal, Blaise (1623–1662). *Pascal's Pensées,* translated
by W. F. Trotter, Introduction by T. S. Eliot.

Pasternak, Boris Leonidovich (1890–1960). *Dr. Zhivago.*
Safe Conduct. I Remember, translated by David Magar-
shack.

Paton, Alan (1903–   ). *Cry, the Beloved Country.*
Tales from a Troubled Land. Too Late the Phalarope.

Pavlov, Ivan Petrovich (1849–1936). *Conditioned Re-*
flexes. Essential Works of Pavlov, edited by Michael
Kaplan. *Essays in Psychology and Psychiatry.*

Peirce, Charles Sanders (1839–1914). *Selected Writings,*
edited by Philip P. Wiener.

Petrarch, Francesco (1304–1374). *Selected Sonnets,*
Odes and Letters, edited by Thomas Goddard Bergin.

Pindar (522?–444 B.C.). *The Odes of Pindar,* translated
by Richard Lattimore.

Pinter, Harold (1930–   ). *The Collection. The Care-*
taker. The Homecoming.

Pirandello, Luigi (1867–1936). *Naked Masks: Five Plays,*
translated by Eric Bentley.

Plato (Aristocles) (427?–347 B.C.). *The Portable Plato,*
edited by Scott Buchanan; or *The Works of Plato,*
translated by Benjamin Jowett, edited by Irwin Ed-
man.

Plautus, Titus Maccius (254?–184 B.C.). *The Haunted House. Six Plays of Plautus*, translated by Lionel Casson.

Pliny the Elder (23–79). *Pliny's Natural History*, edited by Lloyd Haberly.

Poe, Edgar Allan (1809–1849). *Selected Prose and Poetry*, edited by W. H. Auden. *The Narrative of Arthur Gordon Pym*.

Pope, Alexander (1688–1744). *An Essay on Man. Poems of Alexander Pope*, edited by John Butt. *Eloisa to Abelard*.

Pound, Ezra Loomis (1885–   ). *Selected Poems. ABC of Reading. Translations*, Introduction by Hugh Kenner.

Priestley, John Boynton (1894–   ). *The English Comic Characters. The Good Companions. The Doomsday Men*.

Proust, Marcel (1871–1922). *Swann's Way*, translated by C. K. Scott Moncrieff. *Aphorisms and Epigrams from Remembrance of Things Past*, translated and edited by Justin O'Brien.

Pushkin, Alexander (1799–1837). *Eugene Onegin. The Queen of Spades and Other Stories*, translated by Rosemary Edmonds. *Selected Verse*, edited by L. I. Fennell.

Rabelais, François (1495–1553). *The Portable Rabelais*, translated by Samuel Putnam.

Racine, Jean (1639–1699). *Five Plays*, edited by Kenneth Muir.

Renan, Ernest (1823–1892). *The Life of Jesus* (Modern Library).

Renault, Mary (1905–   ). *Bull from the Sea. Charioteer. The King Must Die. Mask of Apollo. Promise of Love*.

Rice, Elmer (1892–1967). *Three Plays*.

Richardson, Samuel (1689–1761). *Clarissa. Pamela*.

Richter, Conrad (1890–   ). *The Fields. The Town. The Trees. The Sea of Grass. The Light in the Forest*.

Roberts, Elizabeth Madox (1886–1941). *Time of Man*,

Introduction by Robert Penn Warren. *Great Meadow*, Afterword by Willard Thorp.

Robinson, Edwin Arlington (1869–1935). *Selected Poems of Edwin Arlington Robinson*, edited by Morton D. Zabel.

Rostand, Edmond (1868–1918). *Cyrano de Bergerac*, translated by Brian Hooker.

Russell, Bertrand Arthur William, Earl (1872–1970). *Principles of Mathematics. Mysticism and Logic. Basic Writings of Bertrand Russell*, edited by R. E. Egner and L. E. Dennon.

Salinger, Jerome David (1919–   ). *Catcher in the Rye. Franny and Zooey. Nine Stories. Raise High the Roof Beam, Carpenter;* and *Seymour an Introduction*.

Sandburg, Carl (1878–1967). *Abraham Lincoln*, 3 vols. *Harvest Poems: Nineteen Ten to Nineteen Sixty. Honey and Salt. Wind Song*.

Santayana, George (1863–1952). *The Last Puritan. Interpretations of Poetry and Religion. Persons and Places. The Sense of Beauty. Skepticism and Animal Faith*.

Sappho (ca. 650 B.C.). *Poems of Sappho*, translated by S. Q. Groden. *Love Songs of Sappho*, translated by P. Roche.

Saroyan, William (1908–   ). *The Time of Your Life and Other Plays*.

Sartre, Jean-Paul (1905–   ). *No Exit and Three Other Plays. The Devil and the Good Lord and Two Other Plays. Essays on Existentialism. The Age of Reason. Nausea. What Is Literature? Saint Genet. The Words*.

Schiller, Friedrich von (1759–1805). *Mary Stuart. William Tell. Love and Intrigue. On the Aesthetic Education of Man. Don Carlos. Wallenstein*.

Schnitzler, Arthur (1862–1931). *Dance of Love*, edited by Eric Bentley.

Schopenhauer, Arthur (1788–1860). *Works of Schopenhauer*, edited by Will Durant, Introduction by Thomas Mann. *World as Will and Representation*, 2 vols., translated by E. F. Payne.

Scott, Sir Walter (1771–1832). *The Fortunes of Nigel. Heart of Mid-Lothian. Ivanhoe. Quentin Durward. Waverley. Lady of the Lake and Other Poems. Life of John Dryden. Rob Roy.*

Seneca, Lucius Annaeus (ca. 4 B.C.–65 A.D.). *Four Tragedies and Octavia. Medea,* translated by Moses Hadas.

Shelley, Percy Bysshe (1792–1822). *Poetical Works,* edited by T. Hutchinson, *Shelley's Critical Prose,* edited by B. R. McElderry, Jr.

Sheridan, Richard Brinsley (1751–1816). *Rivals. School for Scandal.*

Sidney, Sir Philip (1554–1586). *Astrophil and Stella,* edited by M. Putzel. *Selections from Arcadia and Other Poetry and Prose,* edited by T. W. Craik.

Siegel, Eli (1902–). *James and the Children. Hot Afternoons Have Been in Montana: Poems. Hail, American Development. Aesthetic Method in Self-Conflict.*

Sinclair, Upton Beal (1878–1968). *Jungle. Oil. Dragon's Teeth. Cup of Fury.*

Smith, Adam (1723–1790). *Enquiry into the Nature and Causes of the Wealth of Nations,* 2 vols.

Snow, Sir Charles Percy (1905–). *The Search. Strangers and Brothers. The Masters. The New Men. The Light and the Dark. Time of Hope. Corridors of Power. Two Cultures and a Second Look.*

Spinoza, Baruch or **Benedict** (1632–1677). *Ethics: The Road to Inner Freedom. Selections,* edited by J. Wild. *Book of God.*

Staël, Madame de (Anne Louise Germaine Necker) (1766–1817). *Unpublished Correspondence of M. de Staël and the Duke of Wellington,* edited by Victor De Pange, translated by H. Kurtz.

Stein, Gertrude (1874–1946). *Autobiography of Alice B. Toklas. Making of Americans. Picasso. Three Lives.*

Steinbeck, John (1902–). *The Portable Steinbeck. Tortilla Flat. Grapes of Wrath. Cannery Row. Pearl. Travels with Charley. Wayward Bus. East of Eden.*

Stendhal (Marie Henri Beyle) (1783–1842). *Charter-*

house of Parma. Lucien Leuwen, 2 vols. *Private Diaries of Stendhal. The Red and the Black. On Love. A Roman Journal.*

Sterne, Laurence (1713–1768). *Tristram Shandy. A Sentimental Journey through France and Italy and the Journal and Letters to Eliza.*

Stevens, Wallace (1879–1955). *Poems,* edited by Samuel French Morse. *The Necessary Angel.*

Stevenson, Robert Louis (1850–1894). *Treasure Island. Dr. Jekyll and Mr. Hyde. Kidnapped. The Master of Ballantrae. Black Arrow. Child's Garden, of Verse. Great Short Stories of Robert Louis Stevenson.*

Strindberg, August (1849–1912). *Eight Expressionist Plays. Miss Julie. Vasa Trilogy.*

Sumner, William Graham (1840–1910). *Folkways. Conquest of the United States by Spain. Social Darwinism: Selected Essays of William Graham Sumner.*

Swedenborg, Emanuel (1688–1772). *Divine Love and Wisdom. Divine Providence. Heaven and Its Wonders and Hell.*

Synge, John Millington (1871–1909). *Complete Plays of John M. Synge. Aran Islands and Other Writings of John M. Synge.*

Talmud of Jerusalem, edited by D. D. Runes.

Tasso, Torquato (1544–1595). *Jerusalem Delivered.*

Tennyson, Lord Alfred (1809–1892). *Idylls of the King. Poems of Tennyson,* edited by J. H. Buckley.

Terence (Publius Terentius Afer) (185–159 B.C.). *Comedies of Terence,* translated by F. O. Copley.

Thackeray, William Makepeace (1811–1863). *Henry Esmond. Rose and the Ring. Vanity Fair.*

Thomas, Dylan (1914–1953). *Under the Milk Wood. Adventures in the Skin Trade. Beach of Falesa. Quite Early One Morning.*

Thucydides (ca. 455–399 B.C.). *Peloponnesian Wars,* translated by Benjamin Jowett.

Tolstoi, Leo (1828–1910). *Anna Karenina. Childhood, Boyhood, and Youth. Last Diaries. Great Short Works of Leo Tolstoy,* edited by J. Bayley. *Kreutzer Sonata. Resurrection. War and Peace. What Is Art?*

Trilling, Lionel (1905–   ). *Matthew Arnold. E. M. Forster. Experience of Literature. Beyond Culture. Liberal Imagination.*

Trollope, Anthony (1815–1882). *Barchester Towers. Doctor Thorne. Last Chronicle of Barset.*

Trotsky, Leon (1877–1940). *Basic Writings of Trotsky,* edited by I. Deutscher. *Literature and Revolution. Russian Revolution. Terrorism and Communism. Trotsky's Diary in Exile.*

Turgenev, Ivan (1818–1883). *The Vintage Turgenev,* 2 vols. *Three Famous Plays.*

Twain, Mark (Samuel L. Clemens) (1835–1910). *Connecticut Yankee in King Arthur's Court. Innocents Abroad. Prince and the Pauper. Pudd'nhead Wilson. Roughing It. Tom Sawyer Abroad.*

Unamuno, Y Jugo, Miguel de (1864–1936). *Three Exemplary Novels,* translated by Angel Flores. *Abel Sanchez and Other Stories. The Agony of Christianity,* translated by Kurt F. Reinhardt. *Tragic Sense of Life.*

Veblen, Thorstein Bunde (1857–1929). *The Theory of the Leisure Class. The Theory of Business Enterprise. The Instinct of Workmanship. Higher Learning in America. The Engineers and the Price System.*

Vega Carpio, Lope Felix de (1562–1635). *Five Plays.*

Verlaine, Paul (1844–1896). *Selected Poems* (bilingual edition), translated by C. F. MacIntyre. *The Sky Above the Roof,* translated by Brian Hill.

Villon, François (b. 1431). *Complete Works of François Villon* (bilingual edition), translated by Anthony Bonner, Introduction by William Carlos Williams.

Vitruvius, Marcus (Marcus Vitruvius Pollio) (First century B.C.). *The Ten Books on Architecture.*

Warren, Robert Penn (1905–   ). *All The King's Men. Night Rider. Segregation. Wilderness. Band of Angels.*

Waugh, Evelyn (1903–   ). *Bridehead Revisited. Decline and Fall. Handful of Dust. Vile Bodies. Men at Arms* and *Officers and Gentlemen. Helena.*

Weiss, Peter (1916–   ). *The Persecution and Assassination of Jean-Paul Marat as Performed by the Inmates of the Asylum of Charenton under the direction of the Marquis of Sade,* translated by Adrian Mitchell and Geoffrey Skelton. *The Investigation,* translated by J. Swan and U. Grosbard.

Wells, Herbert George (1866–1946). *The Island of Dr. Moreau. The Invisible Man. The War of the Worlds. The First Men in the Moon. The War in the Air* and *In the Days of the Comet* and *The Food of the Gods. The History of Mr. Polly. Tono-Bunguay. Mr. Britling Sees It Through. Joan and Peter. Three Prophetic Novels (When the Sleeper Wakes; Story of Days to Come; The Time Machine).*

Werfel, Franz (1890–1945). *The Forty Days of Musa Dagh. Jacobowsky and the Colonel. The Song of Bernadette.*

West, Rebecca (1892–   ). *The Thinking Reed. The New Meaning of Treason.*

Wharton, Edith (1862–1937). *The Age of Innocence. The House of Mirth. Ethan Frome. Hudson River Bracketed. Roman Fever and Other Stories.*

White, Elwyn Brooks (1899–   ). *E. B. White Reader. One Man's Meat. Second Tree from the Corner.*

Whitehead, Alfred North (1861–1947). *Science and the Modern World. Modes of Thought. Process and Reality. Alfred North Whitehead, An Anthology. Science and Philosophy. Aims of Education and Other Essays. Principia Mathematica* (with Bertrand Russell).

Wilde, Oscar (1854–1900). *Selected Plays. De Profundis. Picture of Dorian Gray. The Selfish Giant.*

Wilder, Thornton (1897–   ). *Three Plays.*

Williams, Tennessee (1911–   ). *The Glass Menagerie. A Streetcar Named Desire.*

Williams, William Carlos (1883–1963). *The Farmers' Daughters: The Collected Stories of William Carlos*

Williams, Introduction by Van Wyck Brooks. *Many Loves: Collected Plays (Many Loves; A Dream of Love; Tituba's Children; The First President). Selected Poems,* Introduction by Randall Jarrell.

Wilson, Edmund (1895–). *Apologies to the Iroquois. Axel's Castle. Galahad* and *I Thought of Daisy. Memoirs of Hecate County. Shades of Light. To the Finland Station.*

Wodehouse, Pelham Grenville (1881–). *Heart of a Goof. Hot Water. Return of Jeeves. How Right You Are* and *Jeeves.*

Wolfe, Thomas Clayton (1900–1938). *The Hills Beyond. From Death to Morning. Look Homeward, Angel. The Lost Boy. Of Time and the River. The Web and the Rock. You Can't Go Home Again.*

Woolf, Virginia (1882–1941). *Common Reader: First Series. A Haunted House and Other Short Stories. Jacob's Room* and *The Waves. Mrs. Dalloway. Orlando. A Room of One's Own. Three Guineas. To the Lighthouse.*

Wordsworth, William (1770–1850). *Poetical Works,* edited by T. Hutchinson. Or *The Prelude, Selected Poems and Sonnets,* edited by Carlos Baker.

Wright, Richard (1908–). *Black Boy. Native Son. Outsider. Uncle Tom's Children. Savage Holiday.*

Yeats, William Butler (1865–1939). *Eleven Plays by William Butler Yeats. Selected Poems of William Butler Yeats. Autobiography of William Butler Yeats.*

Zola, Émile (1840–1902). *L'Assommoir,* translated by A. H. Townsend. *Germinal,* translated by L. W. Tancock. *Nana,* translated by L. Bair.

Appendix A

READING SPEED TEST—PART I
(204 WORDS)

Directions: Read the paragraph below at your usual speed. Be sure that you understand each sentence. Use a watch with a second hand to time yourself. Note the exact position of the second hand when you start reading. As soon as you finish the paragraph, look at your watch. Your score is the number of seconds from start to finish.

Start here: The best readers find that there are some things which they should read slowly. In this way they make sure that they really understand everything they are reading. On certain occasions they do have to read quickly—for example, when they must get information at once, or when they must read a great deal in just a short time. They know that it is a great mistake to try to read everything at the same speed. In reading simple material such as this, they move their eyes along steadily from one group of words to the next. But in reading difficult material, they have to slow down a bit, stop more often to think things over, and take care that they understand everything important. Sometimes their reading rate may be four hundred or more words per minute, at other times less than two hundred words per minute. They know that the greatest mistake of all is to rush through every page so that they miss the main points or misunderstand the author's meaning. These skilled readers prefer to read fifty pages at average speed but with full understanding instead of one hundred pages at high speed but with imperfect or incorrect understanding.

END OF TEST—PART I. Look at your watch. What was your score for Part I?

READING SPEED TEST—PART II
(343 WORDS)

Directions: Read all six paragraphs below at your usual speed. Be sure that you understand each sentence. Use a watch with a second hand to time yourself. Note the exact position of the second hand when you start reading. As soon as you finish all six paragraphs, look at your watch. Your score is the number of seconds from start to finish.

Start here: Over two thousand years ago, a group of men known as the Essenes lived in Palestine. These men did not allow women to join the group, but they did take in children from nearby places. The people owned all property in common, and for this reason there were no rich or poor among them. They believed in God, in Moses his prophet, in the moral law, and in love and justice for all.

The Essenes built a temple to God. Although they did not marry, they allowed their adopted children to do so. Anyone who applied for membership had to give up all his possessions, usually selling them and giving the money to needy members. He had to prove himself to be a man of high character. Every candidate had to wait during a trial period of two years before being accepted as a regular member.

Shortly after the Romans destroyed the city of Jerusalem, the historian Josephus wrote a book *(Wars of the Jews)* in which he described the Essenes as a people who loved everything good and true, hated evil, and lived in close brotherhood. According to Josephus, they were skilled craftsmen and diligent workers. Everyone obeyed the customs of the community, yet the individual enjoyed a great deal of personal freedom.

Among the Essenes the most severe punishment for sins was expulsion, but some of the exiles were eventually forgiven and re-admitted.

Josephus tells us that some of the Essenes permitted members to marry because that was the only way to insure continuance of the community. But the Alexandrian historian Philo insists that they were all forbidden to marry or to beget children, the reason being the desire to avoid any division of loyalty between the family and the entire group.

In recent years archeologists have found and translated the famous Dead Sea Scrolls believed to date back to the time of the Essenes. Certain ideas in these scrolls are like those of the Essenes, and for this reason some scholars believe that they wrote a number of the scrolls.

END OF TEST—PART II. Look at your watch. What was your score for Part II?

Add your scores for Parts I and II. Then compare your total time in seconds with the scores below.

TOTAL SCORES (Parts I and II)	WHAT THE SCORES MEAN
55 or less	Very fast
56–85	Fast
86–115	Average
116–145	Slow
146 or more	Very slow

Appendix B

TEST OF WORD DISCRIMINATION

Directions: Below there are twenty-eight unfinished sentences, each of which ends with a blank space. Each sentence is followed by four words. For each sentence, select the *best one* of the four words to finish the sentence. Write down the twenty-eight words you select.

1. He speaks English very_____.

   plain   neat
   close   well

2. When James was in trouble, he came to us for _____.

   help   thanks
   pain   rewards

3. I could not hear her words because she spoke too _____.

   slowly   wisely
   nicely   quietly

4. Fred voted in the election because he considered voting to be a_____.

   mistake   duty
   desire   skill

5. The widow's large gifts to the poor proved her to be rich and_____.

   careless   ungrateful
   generous   reliable

215

6. The journey took much longer than any of us
_____.

regretted   realized
doubted   deserved

7. Joan spoke about her friend's stupid actions in words
of utter_____.

gratitude   praise
courtesy   contempt

8. I warned our driver that in winter the roads would be
extremely_____.

complicated   distant
disturbing   dangerous

9. A patient who refuses to take his medicine will have
to suffer the_____.

costs   disappointment
consequences   rewards

10. Everyone present voted for the bill except Philip,
who voted in_____.

opposition   support
favor   agreement

11. The weeping mother of the wounded child wrung
her hands in_____.

despair   vigilance
safety   joy

12. With hundreds of spies in our midst, we must realize
that the price of our liberty is constant_____.

prosperity   vigilance
agreement   disaster

13. Paying no attention to William, Jane treated him
with complete_____.

attention   indifference
devotion   recognition

14. Among all the people I met in my travels, he was the strangest person I ever_____.

reconsidered   miscalculated
ignored   encountered

15. For the defense a new attorney presented the _____.

arraignment   conviction
evidence   verdict

16. Since he and I agreed on everything, his comments on what I said were naturally_____.

positive   critical
negative   contradictory

17. These unexpected events annoyed me so much that I became quite_____.

exasperated   important
ridiculous   reassured

18. Since we were humble and loyal citizens, we greeted our king's representative with_____.

scorn   deference
violence   humiliation

19. The young lady became so confused that her peculiar statements no longer seemed_____.

unreasonable   absurd
rational   baffling

20. Fred lost his grip and fell from the ladder_____.

mercifully   continuously
brazenly   precipitately

21. I trust, sir, that your gross error will not have serious _____.

reversals   repercussions
modifications   advantages

22. Although the inventor worked very well alone, eventually he agreed to accept_____.

    detractors   opportunists
    collaborators   honoraria

23. The author's manuscript had to be rejected because of its numerous_____.

    qualifications   qualities
    attributes   infelicities

24. Our attorney fortunately discovered a fraudulent clause whereby the contract was_____.

    validated   modified
    vitiated   misconstrued

25. In my statistical tables some important figures were missing and had to be_____.

    interposed   interpolated
    restricted   retroverted

26. Reflecting her impatience and anger, Mary's retort was_____.

    considerate   judicious
    verbose   vitriolic

27. William was a man of parts, expert in many pursuits, therefore a man of_____.

    versatility   credibility
    impenetrability   specialization

28. The serious charges of the plaintiff against the defendant have yet to be_____.

    differentiated   substantiated
    pre-empted   disentangled

END OF TEST. Compare your answers with the printed answers on page 223. Your score is the number right. Compare your score with the scores below.

SCORES	WHAT THE SCORES MEAN
24–28	Excellent
19–23	Very good
14–18	Good
9–13	Fair
0–8	Poor

Appendix C

TEST OF PARAGRAPH MEANING

Directions: Below there are five paragraphs, each of which is followed by two questions. Read each paragraph only once but carefully. For each question, select and write down the best answer. Your answer should be based on the paragraph.

PARAGRAPH I

A story which is untrue but well written will keep us interested while we are reading it. We forget the untrue parts and follow the plot with eager enthusiasm if the events and characters are lifelike.

1. Paragraph I is about
    a. philosophy
    b. fiction
    c. science

2. Paragraph I tells us that a skillful author can
    a. write clearly and concisely
    b. make dead things come alive
    c. make imaginary events seem real

PARAGRAPH II

Our community is confronted with serious difficulties. There are economic hardships, which include unemployment and inflation. There is a high incidence of mental illness. The most urgent difficulties, however, are those of racial antagonism and conflict.

3. Paragraph II is about
    a. a corrupt society
    b. social problems
    c. the medical profession

4. Paragraph II tells us that in our community there are serious
    a. economic, psychological, and moral shortcomings
    b. programs to alleviate unemployment and illness
    c. failures in science and education

PARAGRAPH III

Newspapers, magazines, and books often contain maps which help the reader to understand the information being presented. Too many readers are unfamilar with the sizes and locations of continents, countries, cities, rivers, and other physical features involved in historical events. Maps supplement and illuminate the reading material so that the reader can easily see how geography affects history.

5. Paragraph III is about
   a. mapmaking as a science
   b. the purpose of maps
   c. the reason why geography is difficult for most readers

6. Paragraph III tells us that maps are useful because the information in them
   a. helps readers to understand events
   b. is usually accurate
   c. cannot be found in books

PARAGRAPH IV

The skin consists of two main portions. These are the epidermis or upper portion and the corium or deeper portion. There are four layers of cells but no blood vessels in the epidermis. The corium (also called the dermis) has an upper layer of cells extending into the epidermis and a lower layer of cells made up of white fibers and elastic tissue.

7. Paragraph IV is about
   a. functions of the skin
   b. the nature of cells
   c. the structure of skin

8. Paragraph IV tells us that
   a. the deeper part of the skin has two layers of cells
   b. the upper part of the skin is made of elastic tissue
   c. there are no blood vessels in the dermis

PARAGRAPH V

Scientific experiments in psychology and other sciences depend upon certain well-established steps or techniques.

These include accurate observation, the collection and organization of pertinent facts, the development of hypotheses and tentative theories, and the verification of theories by application of them under controlled conditions. The experimenter compares the behavior of a control group with that of his experimental group. In this way he attempts to discover the factor which causes the differences in the behavior of the two groups.

9. Paragraph V is about
    a. the prejudices of scientists
    b. methods of scientific investigation
    c. socially desirable control of group behavior

10. Paragraph V tells us
    a. the limitations of science as a set of theories
    b. why it is necessary to conduct experiments in psychology
    c. scientific research methods which disclose laws of behavior

END OF TEST. Compare your answers with the printed answers on page 223. Your score is the number right. Compare your score with the scores below.

SCORES	WHAT THE SCORES MEAN
10	Excellent
8 or 9	Very good
6 or 7	Good
4 or 5	Fair
3 or less	Poor

Answers For Tests

TEST OF WORD DISCRIMI-NATION

TEST OF PARAGRAPH MEANING

1. well	1. b
2. help	2. c
3. quietly	3. b
4. duty	4. a
5. generous	5. b
6. realized	6. a
7. contempt	7. c
8. dangerous	8. a
9. consequences	9. b
10. opposition	10. c
11. despair	
12. vigilance	
13. indifference	
14. encountered	
15. evidence	
16. positive	
17. exasperated	
18. deference	
19. rational	
20. precipitately	
21. repercussions	
22. collaborators	
23. infelicities	
24. vitiated	
25. interpolated	
26. vitriolic	
27. versatility	
28. substantiated	

INDEX

(For authors of special books in literature, philosophy, psychology, religion, science, and the arts, see alphabetical lists on pages 190–211.)